DURHAM RAILWAYS

CHARLIE EMETT

SUTTON PUBLISHING LIMITED

Sutton Publishing Limited
Phoenix Mill · Thrupp · Stroud ·
Gloucestershire · GL5 2BU

First published 1999

Copyright © Charlie Emett, 1999

Title page photograph: A plaque at the
North Road Railway Museum, Darlington,
showing the men who started a transport
revolution.

British Library Cataloguing in Publication Data
A catalogue record for this book is available from
the British Library.

ISBN 0-7509-2076-9

Typeset in 10/11 Bembo.
Typesetting and origination by
Sutton Publishing Limited.
Printed in Great Britain by
Ebenezer Baylis, Worcester.

ACKNOWLEDGEMENTS

My thanks to Andrew Smith, editor of the *Northern Echo*, can never be adequate to honour my debt to him for giving me the freedom to search through this excellent newspaper's picture library, always a most enjoyable occupation. Very special thanks to the guardians of those *Echo* archives, Peter Chapman and two clever ladies of great charm and loveliness, Jane Whitfield and Christine Watson. Your help, advice and coffee are much appreciated. What an efficient trio you make! To the dedicated staff of Darlington Railway Centre and Museum, to the Ken Hoole Study Centre, and in particular Ann Wilson, I give thanks for responding so quickly and positively to my queries. Richard Barber, your knowledge of railway matters is encyclopedic and I thank you for sharing some of it with me. You have done another fine transformation job with my manuscript, Ellen Rutter – thanks for the typing. How reassuring it is to know that the editorial side is in the safe hands of the editors, Simon Fletcher, Alison Flowers and Joyce Percival, and that Rebecca Nicholls is dealing with my publicity. With such knowledge I can sleep well at night, my grateful thanks to you, my friends at Sutton Publishing. You are a brilliant team and working with you is a delight. I apologise to anyone I have inadvertently overlooked; and would point out that any errors are mine.

An early London and North Eastern Railway poster depicting Thomas Hackworth's locomotive
Coronation built to commemorate the coronation of King William IV in 1831.

CONTENTS

The interior of the cab of ex–Stockton and Darlington Railway locomotive 0–6–0 No. 1275.

INTRODUCTION

The railway age began during the afternoon of Thursday 23 May 1822, when 300 shouting, singing navvies dragged a carriage containing one of the local dignitaries into Stockton where, at St John's Well, he laid the first rail of the Stockton and Darlington Railway. Afterwards everyone sang 'God Save The King', the dignitaries, including representatives of the proposed Liverpool and Manchester and Leeds and Hull Railways, Mr Meynell (first chairman of the Stockton and Darlington Railway) and George Stephenson, went to the Mayor's reception and the navvies dined on bread, cheeses and ale at the Black Lion Inn.

For centuries the word 'rail' has been used to denote a strip of wood. When parallel strips were used to ease the passage of coal carts over rough ground they were called rails and formed a 'rail-way', which became the general term for tramway, plateway and wagonway, all of which were virtually synonymous. However, there were differences: a tramway was usually on a sloped plateway on which wheels with flat treads could move; a railway came to mean an altogether different kind of track that required the wheels to be flanged. The earliest railways were privately owned and used solely by the owner to carry his goods mostly over his own land.

In 1804, Captain Blackett, who owned Wylam Colliery in County Durham, had a locomotive built by John Whinfield of Gateshead. It weighed only 4½ tons and had flanged wheels and Blackett, realising that it would be too heavy for his wooden rails, had the wheels removed and used it to drive machinery. When, in 1808, the wooden rails at his Wylam Colliery railway wore out, Blackett replaced them with cast-iron plate rails and his colliery manager, William Hedley, constructed a four-wheeled carriage operated by four men turning handles to move it along pulling loaded wagons. The experiment was not a success and so Hedley mounted an engine on the carriage, which worked but tended to be short of steam.

Hedley designed and the colliery blacksmith, Timothy Hackworth, built two large engines, *Puffing Billy* and *Wylam Dilly*, a year later. Weighing about 8 tons each, they were far too heavy for the plate rails and were therefore mounted on eight wheels to spread the load, and worked satisfactorily. When the plate rails were replaced by end plates, the locomotives were rebuilt to the original, four-wheeled design, now with flanges. Following a disagreement about working Sundays, Hackworth left Wylam Colliery and after gaining further experience elsewhere, went on to design and build locomotives for the Stockton and Darlington Railway. Although engine design developed steadily, the wagons they were to pull remained essentially the same as horse-drawn versions.

George Stephenson was born in Wylam in 1781 and moved with his family to Killingworth where he was employed in a colliery, rising to be an engineman. Realising that a faster means of moving coal had to be found, he produced a mobile steam engine in June 1814, which he called *Blucher*. It could pull eight loaded wagons weighing 30 tons at 4 mph. Working with Dodd and Losh, an iron-founder who owned Walter Iron Works, he developed a method of turning locomotive wheels using chains that ran over toothed wheels on each axle. These became a hallmark of George Stephenson design.

The Stockton and Darlington Railway was officially opened on 27 September 1825, when Locomotive No. 1 hauled twenty-six wagons and a coach the 21 miles from near West Auckland to Stockton, the remaining six leaving the procession at Darlington. The opening set the pattern for the development of a railway system that would spread worldwide. Earlier that year, on 1 January, George Stephenson and Son was launched for the purpose of engineering and railway surveying. George and Robert Stephenson and their partners were by this time well established as locomotive builders and railway engineers. The railway had become an industry in its own right and the expansion of the railway system beyond the requirements of localised industry could now begin.

However, no birth is painless, and that of the Stockton and Darlington locomotive was almost aborted. Although the line had a flamboyant opening, teething troubles soon developed. Within a month there was a shortage of wagons and 150 of those in use were, according to Thomas Storey, the railway's resident engineer, 'as bad a set of wagons as were ever turned out on a railway'.

By May 1826, the company possessed four locomotives, all built to the same pattern. They pulled between twenty and twenty-four wagons on a regular basis, carrying up to 92 tons, from Brussleton Plane to Stockton in 4 hours, returning with empties in 5 hours, including an hour spent in stoppages. Between 500 and 600 tons per week were hauled, equal to the work of twelve to fourteen horses in the same circumstances. But the inclines were difficult to negotiate and often locomotives were stood, waiting for a build-up of steam. Poor performance was compounded by abuse from careless drivers. Everything considered, the locomotives were simply not equipped to carry out the work demanded of them; and, in 1827, serious consideration was given to abandoning them in favour of horses. However, in 1830, Hackworth designed an engine specifically for passenger traffic. Built by Robert Stephenson and called *Globe*, it could, if conditions were right, reach a speed of 50 mph. By 1832, horse haulage could no longer be justified and in August 1833 it was decided that it should be terminated on the Stockton and Darlington main line.

Altogether, some seventeen separate railways came into being throughout Durham between 1828 and 1894. The first, the Clarence Railway, was promoted as the Tees and Weardale Railway but was renamed to honour the Duke of Clarence, later King William IV.

Built under the wayleaves system and authorised by a Deed of Settlement, of 3 February 1834, the Stanhope and Tyne Railway opened from Stanhope to Annfield on 15 May 1834. An extension to South Shields was opened on 15 September that year. Seven years later the company became insolvent and on 5 February 1841 was dissolved. The eastern section, from Leadgate to South Shields, was incorporated into the Pontop and South Shields Railway and on 23 May 1842 the western section was sold to the Derwent Iron Company to carry limestone from quarries at Stanhope to the steelworks at Consett. From 1 January 1845 it was leased by the S&DR and on 22 July 1847 was sold to the Wear Valley Railway.

On 13 August 1834, authority was given for the Durham and Sunderland Railway to be built between the two towns with a branch to Haswell, but only the branch materialised. It opened on 5 July 1836 for mineral traffic, and for passengers on 30 August of that year.

Against bitter opposition from the Stockton and Darlington Railway, the West Durham Railway was built from an end on junction with the Clarence Railway. It was constructed, at first relying on wayleaves, then, when well advanced and with the benefit of an Act of Parliament, was passed on 4 July 1839. The line opened from Willington to Byers Green on 12 June 1840 and was extended to Whitemee Colliery, north of Crook, on 19 October.

It took two Acts of Parliament to authorise the Great North of England Railway, a line from Newcastle to York. In 1839, the Croft branch of the S&DR was bought, although only its northern end was used. The line opened for mineral traffic on 1 January 1841 and for passengers on 30 March. A branch line to Richmond was opened on 10 September 1846.

An extension of the S&DR from Soho, near Shildon, through Shildon tunnel, was opened to South Church on 19 April 1842, and to Crook on 8 November 1843. It was called the Bishop Auckland and Weardale Railway. The Weardale Extension Railway extended it and it was bought by the Wear Valley Railway on 22 July 1847.

The Newcastle and Darlington Junction Railway was incorporated on 18 June 1842, opened on 18 June 1844 and planned to run a service from 1 January 1845 but had no engines. The GNER agreed to supply some along with rolling stock but would not staff the line. Despite this inauspicious start the company expanded: the Durham Junction Railway was acquired in 1844 and the Brandling Junction Railway in 1845. The Durham and Sunderland and the Pontop, South Shields Railways and the Wearmouth Dock Company were added in 1846. That year, under an Act of Parliament of 27 July, the powers of the GNER over its northern end were transferred to the N&DJR, although that company remained independent until 1850.

The Wear Valley Railway, an 11-mile branch from the Bishop Auckland and Weardale Railway to Frosterley with a branch to Bishopley Crag, was opened on 3 August 1847. The Wear Valley Extension Railway opened on 21 October 1895, but by then the mineral traffic at Wearhead was in decline. Therefore, its power was transferred to the NER on 31 July 1894.

Running from a junction with the S&DR at Hopetown, north of Darlington, sanctioned on 3 July 1854 and opened on 8 July 1856, the Darlington and Barnard Castle Railway became part of the cross-Pennine route between Durham and the steelworks of west Cumberland. The company amalgamated with the S&DR on 23 July 1858.

On 30 July 1855, authority was given for a short line to be built along the Dearness Valley, west of Darlington, to join Waterhouses with the East Hedleyhope Colliery. It opened in 1858 for goods, and for passengers on 1 November 1877.

On 17 July 1857, authority was given for a line from Spring Garden Junction, near West Auckland, to Tebay, via Barnard Castle, to carry coke from Durham to the Cumberland steelworks. It opened for mineral traffic on 4 July 1861 and was formally opened on 7 August, the public using it from the next day.

Authorised on 28 June 1861, the Frosterley and Stanhope Railway, an extension of the Wear Valley Railway, although nominally independent, was sponsored by the S&DR, which absorbed all 2½ miles of it on 30 June 1862. It opened for mineral traffic on 30 April and for passenger traffic on 22 October of that year.

The Forcett Railway was an independent line that branched south from the D&BCR east of Gainford to quarries near Forcett. It was opened in October 1866. Another line branching south from the D&BCR was the Merrybent and Darlington Railway. Opened on 11 June 1870 to serve quarries, it was soon in financial difficulties and was wound up on 17 June 1878.

By 1890, over 85 per cent of the total mileage of railway track throughout the whole of Britain had been constructed, and the impact on Victorian society was tremendous. The railways had reached their zenith in popular esteem with more travelling by train, either on business or for pleasure, than ever before. Most of the railways had strong territorial associations, regional loyalty thrived and railway issues, in particular steam locomotives, constantly stimulated public interest.

In 1921, there were 120 independent railways throughout Britain. That year, as a result of the Railways Act, all these were merged to form four large companies: GNR, LMS, LNER, and SR. Those companies left out of this grouping became Independent and Joint. The grouping took effect from 1 January 1923.

The demand for coal, which had been the stimulus behind the opening of the S&DR in 1825, was at an all-time low by 1931. Coal traffic was the lifeblood of the railways, especially the LNER, which serviced many coalfields, including those throughout Durham, and the associated heavy engineering and shipbuilding concerns that had sprung up along Durham's three main rivers, the Tees, Wear and Tyne. The effect of the slump on these industries was both immediate and dramatic. It brought a severe depression in rail traffic and the LNER was the most acutely affected of the 'Big Four'.

However, the LNER weathered the slump in a most remarkable way. It set about improving passenger train services on its main lines to satisfy an insatiable public demand. Streamliners like *Silver Link* were used on restricted routes, and an average of 70 per cent of all of the LNER journeys were completed either on time or ahead of schedule.

Most of the locomotives working throughout the Durham network were locally built. They pulled easily recognisable non-corridor clerestory roofed coaches that had been designed by David Bain in about 1900. Sir Nigel Gresley, Chief Engineer first for GNR and then LNER, was a remarkable man with an enquiring and receptive mind. Among his many accomplishments, he designed the first of the 'Shire' class engines, No. 234, *Yorkshire*, 4–4–0, which was built at Darlington. This remarkable man deserves the accolade for overseeing the continuous development of his first 'Pacific' class engine, *Great Northern*, to finally produce the A4 class *Mallard*. Built in 1938, it holds the world steam speed record at 126 mph.

The overall level of LNER services continued to improve and expand during 1938, the main development being the introduction of a new 'Flying Scotsman' service, which had restaurant cars. With the LNER, passenger comfort was of paramount importance. The development of services continued steadily until, on 3 September 1939, war was declared on Germany and priorities changed. The 'Big Four' companies had been aware of this likelihood for some time, and were well prepared to meet the challenges of this dire situation. The Emergency Powers Defence Act of August 1939 empowered the Ministry of Transport to take over all forms of transport, which was put into effect by the Emergency (Railway Control) Order of 1 September 1939, when the Minister took control of the 'Big Four'.

The severe winter of 1940 played havoc with rail services; on 19 February 1941 a snow storm developed which, over several days, increased in severity and caused many derailments and accidents. Throughout Durham, as elsewhere, telegraph wires were brought down. All northbound trains were terminated at Darlington, while southbound trains were re-routed via the LMS. Rather carelessly, the LNER actually managed to lose several expresses.

As the war progressed, so the demand for coal and coke increased and the Durham coalfields and others were kept to full capacity. This caused major problems in getting the freight trains to their destinations without conflicting with other services. The 'Big Four' had proved their worth during the Second World War – by the end of it they were exhausted. Locomotives, rolling stock, track, infrastructure and personnel were all worn out.

On 1 April 1946, the Ministry of War Transport was abolished and civilian control of the railways resumed under a new Transport Ministry headed by Alfred Barnes. On 1 January 1948, the railway was nationalised, becoming British Rail and bringing to an end the comparatively short era of the 'Big Four' companies. Commenting on this transition, one wag suggested that now all the 'Expresses' (then a Tory newspaper) should be renamed 'Heralds' (then a Labour newspaper). The Transport Act of 1947 that introduced this change paid little regard to commercial considerations. The idea behind it was that the co-ordination of all forms of transport would provide the public service that the country needed and from it profit would naturally flow. At this time the railway was vital to the country, which was still recovering from the hardships brought about by war.

When the Conservatives gained power in 1951, the attitude to the country's transport system changed and competition became the most important factor in the running of the railways. However, there were complications. Bound by the 1947 Transport Act, BR still had to accept all goods offered, whether profit-making or not, and the prices of freight and passenger traffic were fixed. Also, road transport, express coaches and private cars were making inroads into rail traffic business. By the mid-1950s BR was deemed by many to have run its course.

The Modernisation Plan of 1955 was produced to re-invigorate technical developments and improvements with an injection of £1,200 million, which was to be spent over fifteen years to modernise the system completely. This would entail the extension of electrified routes and the replacement of nearly 20,000 steam engines with electric and diesel locomotives. The difference between the diesel-electric and the wholly electric locomotive is that the diesel-electric is self-contained. It carries its own power house, a diesel engine that drives an electric generator. The wholly electric locomotive picks up its electrical energy from rails or wires beside or above the track. It marked the beginning of the end for steam railways. The last of the main line steam engines was in regular service in 1968.

Until recently, the railways were common carriers and had to carry anything that was offered. Now the freight side concentrates mainly on the transportation of bulk loads. Today's express passenger train is a vastly superior form of transport to any other. With its all-steel, air-conditioned carriages and automatic doors between them, it offers everything its competitors have except videos and traffic jams. The day may not be long in coming when the star attraction on Durham railways will be the automatic, driverless train. Even with today's advanced technology, no other form of transport can match that.

CHAPTER ONE

THE STOCKTON AND DARLINGTON RAILWAY

The S&DR was not the world's first public railway – the Loughborough and Nanpanton was in 1789. It was not the first steam railway – the Penydarren Colliery line, South Wales, which carried VIP passengers at its opening was. Also, it was not the first passenger railway – the Swansea and Mumbles in 1806 was. It was not even the first railway instituted by an Act of Parliament – the Middleton Railway, Leeds, 1758, which switched entirely to steam in 1812, holds that distinction. But it was the first public railway worked by steam, although for several years after the gala opening of 1825 its steam traction was reserved for freight.

This composite picture illustrates the transition from horse-drawn colliery wagons to those drawn by steam power. George Stephenson (1781–1848) (right), and his son, Robert (1803–59) (centre), were engineers associated with the early development of railways. George built his first locomotive in 1814 for a colliery tramway. He became the engineer to both the S&DR and the Liverpool & Manchester line, for which he persuaded the directors to use steam. In 1827, after three years in South America, Robert returned to manage his father's engine works in Wylam where the *Rocket* was built. Timothy Hackworth, on the left, the foreman smith at Wylam when *Puffing Billy* was built, was appointed resident engineer and manager of the S&DR. Hackworth's first locomotive built to his own design was the *Royal George*. Unlike the earlier locomotives which were festooned with rods and levers over the boiler, the *Royal George* had none. Moreover, its 15 ton weight was spread across six wheels. *Locomotion*, famous for hauling the first train on the S&DR had its weight of 8 tons spread across four wheels.

This model depicts *Locomotion* hauling some 600 people in 38 chaldrons and 1 passenger coach, the first ever, *Experiment*, across the River Skerne, Darlington, at the official opening of the S&DR on 27 September 1825. It captures the spirit of the event perfectly. The coach had three windows on each side but no springs and could accommodate up to eighteen passengers seated on longitudinal, wooden seats. It left much to be desired, but it was a start.

In May 1975, as part of the 150th S&DR celebrations, the replica of *Locomotion* went to Beamish Open Air Museum, near Chester-le-Street, to feature in a television news report. This is the first day of shooting and Mike Satow is at the controls.

A commemorative plate depicting *Locomotion* and produced for the 150th S&DR celebrations.

The horse-drawn chaldrons featured on this Clarence Railway Company plate mark the end of an era.

The Royal George was built in 1827 and is seen in detail on this mug. The engine shows how much and how quickly Timothy Hackworth advanced locomotive design.

A cavalcade of locomotives to mark the 150th anniversary of the beginning of the railways on 27 September 1825. Thirty-five engines took part, including the latest British Rail high-speed train. The procession was proudly headed by an identical replica of *Locomotion*, seen here.

RAILWAYS 1825·1975

Stephenson's Locomotion
7ᵖ
1825 Stockton and Darlington Railway

Waverley Class **8**ᵖ
1876 North British Railway Drummond

Caerphilly Castle **10**ᵖ
1923 Great Western Railway Castle Class

High-Speed Train **12**ᵖ
1975 British Rail Inter-City Service HST

In 1975, the Post Office issued a commemorative set of stamps to mark the development of railways from Stephenson's *Locomotion*, through the steam era to today's less romantic but much more expensive high-speed train.

The *Evening Despatch* personality girl, nineteen-year-old Yvonne Gallop of Normanby, stands beneath a lamp from Cockfield railway station on the *Northern Echo* display stand at the S&DR 150th Railway Exhibition at the Magnet Bowl, Darlington, on 16 August 1975. Darlington was chosen as the headquarters of the *Northern Echo* because it had excellent railway communications, which enabled copies to be sold simultaneously in London and Edinburgh, and made it a regional newspaper in the widest possible sense.

As part of the Rail 150 Exhibition that opened on Monday 25 August 1975, the name *George Stephenson* was conferred on this LMS class 5 MT 4–6–0 locomotive No. 4767 by the Rt Hon. William Whitelaw, CH, MC, MP. In all, 842 of these Stanier-designed engines were built by LMS. Often described as their most successful engine, the first was introduced in 1934. This magnificent locomotive excelled both on freight and express passenger duties. Ian Storey is on the right of the picture.

O.V.S. Bulleid, who became head of locomotive design for the Southern Railway in 1937, designed this 'Merchant Navy' class 4–6–2 locomotive 35028 *Clan Line*. It came into service in 1948 and represents the ultimate design for passenger tender locomotives of the Southern Railway. One of the routes 'Merchant Navy' class locomotives travelled when working enthusiast specials was the East Coast line as far north as Newcastle.

In 1839, Robert Stephenson and Co. built the original *Evening Star*, which had two driving wheels, for the GWR. *Evening Star* was also the name given to the last steam locomotive built for British Rail in 1960 and it is seen here. It is a class 9F 2–10–0 No. 92220, and this one has ten driving wheels.

Green Arrow, seen here just outside Shildon on 25 August 1975, is a class V2 2–6–2 No. 4771 built in 1936. It was one of five constructed as forerunners of a new class designed to meet the ever increasing demands for fast, reliable, mixed traffic locomotives. *Green Arrow* regularly hauled the 3.55 p.m. 'Scottish Goods' north from London. At the outbreak of the Second World War almost 100 class V2s were in service and LNER crews called them 'the locomotives that won the war'. In total, 182 were built.

Introduced in 1938, *Cookham Manor*, a GWR 'Manor' class 4–6–0 No. 7808 locomotive, seen here on 25 August 1975, was designed for use on secondary lines using parts from 2–6–0 engines. It is seen here at Heighington station.

Gordon, class 9F 2–10–0 No. 600, seen here on 25 August 1975, was the second locomotive of its class, 'Austerity', to be built by the Ministry of Supply for use by the British Army on the Longmoor Military Railway in Hampshire for instruction purposes. It was introduced in 1943 and named after General Gordon of Khartoum. Its wartime livery was blue. It is seen here towing London Transport Electric No. 12 *Sarah Siddons*.

The Bishop of Wakefield, the Rt Revd Dr Eric Treacy, a lifelong railway enthusiast, led a footplate fellowship from the tender of *Locomotion* at Bank Top Station, Darlington, at the S&DR's 150th anniversary, Sunday 31 August 1975. Here he walks past *Mayflower*, LNER class B1 4–6–0 No. 1306, which was introduced in 1948. The name *Mayflower* was originally carried by its sister locomotive, No. 61379.

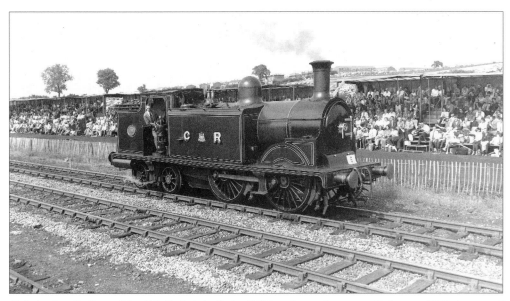

Caledonian Railway No. 419 0–4–4, built in 1907 and seen here on 25 August 1975, is one of ninety-one class 439 locomotives built between 1900 and 1925. Its livery is pale blue, the colour used by Caledonian Railways on their locomotives before 1923 when the company was absorbed into the LMR. It is seen here at the 150th S&DR anniversary and was part of the procession.

Seen here being coaled in the coalyard of the Dunn Bros of Shildon in readiness for the 150th-anniversary cavalcade at 8 a.m. on Sunday 31 August 1975, is *Cookham Manor*, GWR class 'Manor' 4–6–0 No. 7808 which came into service in 1938. This lightweight, modern, two-cylinder, passenger locomotive, along with others of the 'Manor' class, marked the completion of the GWR standardisation policy of the 4–6–0 type steam locomotives for passenger service.

Les Dunn and his brothers provided all the labour for coaling the exhibition's locomotives free of charge during the firm's annual holiday. The locomotive being coaled is LMS class 4MT 2–6–0 No. 43106. This most handsome of locomotives was designed by the last Chief Mechanical Engineer of the LMS, H.G. Ivatt, and came into service in 1951. No attempt has been made to streamline it, the wheels are in full view and there is no cover below the smokebox. In 1966, it worked a freight to Kirkby Stephen, two years before being withdrawn.

Leading the line-up at Shildon in this picture is LNWR 'Precedent' class 2–4–0 No. 790 *Hardwicke* which was introduced in 1873, and seen here on 25 August 1975. In the summer of 1895, at the time of intense rivalry between the West Coast route (London and North Western Railway and the Caledonian Railway) and the East Coast route (Great Northern Railway, North Eastern Railway and the North British Railway), *Hardwicke* raced the section from Crewe to Carlisle. Her finest performance was on 22 August 1895 when she covered 141 miles in 126 minutes. This included a climb over Shap summit at an average speed of 62.4 mph. Her regular crew were Driver B. Dobinson and Fireman W. Wolstencroft. LMS 'Compound' class 4–4–0 No. 1000, introduced in 1902, was the first locomotive of 'Compound' design. 'Compounds' worked throughout the whole of the Midland system and in Scotland during the LMS days and some 240 of them were built.

During the 150th S&DR celebrations, Caledonian Railway class 439 0–4–4T No. 419 introduced in 1907, was used to shuttle spectators between Shildon and the marshalling yard. The class 439 was developed from a locomotive designed by Dugald Drummond in 1884.

LNER class D49 4–4–0 No. 246 *Morayshire* is seen here at Shildon shed shunting LNER class V2 2–6–2 No. 4771 *Green Arrow*. Introduced in 1927, *Morayshire* was one of seventy-six D49 class locomotives, about half of which were named after the counties through which LNER traffic was worked. The remainder were named after famous Fox Hunter packs, the class being known as 'Shires' or 'Hunts'.

The S&DR 150th-anniversary cavalcade being marshalled at Shildon. The locomotive on the left is LMS class 5MT 4–6–0 No. 4767 *George Stephenson*. Introduced in 1947, it was one of 842 Stanier-designed locomotives, which were first introduced in 1934. No. 2238, on the right, was introduced in 1918, one of Sir Vincent Raven's NER class T2 0–8–0 locomotives, of which 120 were built between 1913 and 1918.

GWR class 'Modified Hall' 4–6–0 No. 6960 *Raveningham Hall*, introduced in 1949, was one of a class that eventually numbered 330. *Raveningham Hall* almost never reached Shildon for the 150th anniversary cavalcade because, *en route*, its bearings seized up at Northallerton. When it did arrive its livery was the correct colour, green, but the shade was far too light.

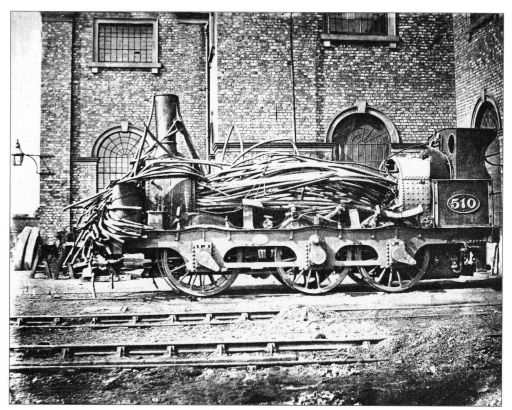

In 1933, this 0–6–0 locomotive No. 510 got all steamed up about something and blew her top! There is a moral here somewhere.

The men who built the S&DR, the railway navvies, carved out of the English countryside a new iron-age architecture of unparalleled grandeur and audacity as they blasted, tunnelled and drank their uncouth way across respectable England. This anarchic elite was preached at and plundered, sworn at and swindled and had to endure many perils and disasters while much of the glory went to the engineers and much of the profit to the entrepreneurs. Using picks and shovels, wheelbarrows, horses and gunpowder, they built a railway system that established cheap, fast travel, encouraged ideas and commerce and did much to create Britain's national prosperity and international ascendancy.

This famous painting of *Locomotion* pulling some thirty-eight chaldrons and the very first passenger coach, *Experiment*, over the Skerne Bridge at Darlington during the opening of the S&DR was based on a contemporary sketch. It was altered slightly to depict the second *Experiment*, not the first one, but the spirit of the event is retained.

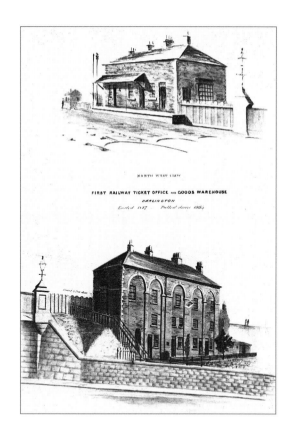

Near Skerne Bridge, a small goods warehouse, transformed into a booking office, waiting room and cottage together with a narrow wooden platform, sufficed as Darlington's station from 1833 until 1842. It was approached by a flight of steps from the east side of North Road. North Road station, believed to be the oldest purpose-built railway station in the world, replaced it. North Road station is west of North Road, not actually on it.

The forecourt of Darlington's North Road station and some of the staff, *c.* 1900.

Class 06 0–8–0 No. 63366 entering North Road station on 27 March 1963.

Northern Gas Board's No. 1 locomotive *Tempus Fugit* dominates this picture taken at North Road Station, 4 April 1988. The station had become a railway museum by this time.

No. 910, an express passenger class 2–4–0 locomotive, was built in 1874, one of fifty-five similar locomotives built for the LNER between 1872 and 1882. It worked for almost fifty years before being withdrawn from service in January 1925.

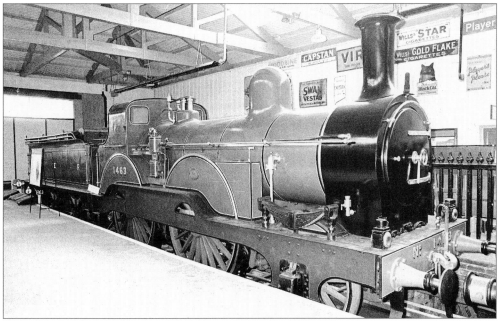

In 1885 NER produced another express passenger class 2–4–0, No. 1463, one of twenty built, all of which survived to become LNER class E5. Designed by a committee chaired by NER General Manager, Henry Tennant, the locomotives of this class were usually called 'Tennants'. They were built at Darlington's North Road workshops. No. 1463 was withdrawn from service in 1927 and later restored; it is seen here in its permanent home, North Road Railway Museum, in about 1990.

The NER emblem. The S&DR was the curtain-raiser to the full flowering, in 1923, of what Sir John Clapham termed 'The Early Railway Age'. That year Parliament decreed that 120 independent railway companies should be merged into groups, seven of which would become the LNER. Three of these groups, the Great Northern Railway, the North Eastern and the North British, had long cooperated in maintaining the services along the East Coast route from Kings Cross to Scotland. The NER was the largest and strongest of the three because of the volume of freight and mineral traffic generated in the industrial areas and the steady west-to-east flow of coal from the mines to the east-coast ports for shipment. Its proud lineage had its genesis at the beginning of the railway age when the opening of the Stockton and Darlington in 1825 created the image of public, as distinct from private, railways operated by steam locomotives.

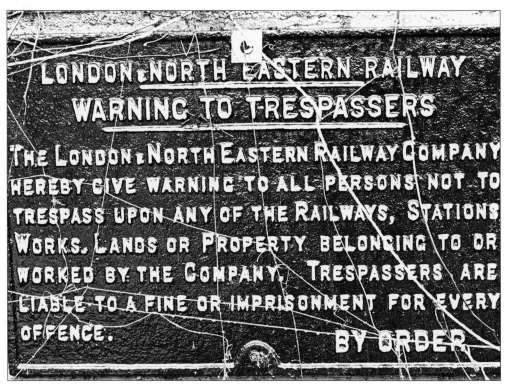

The LNER came into being on 1 January 1923, one of four large companies formed as a direct consequence of the Railways Act of 1921. It was managed in a completely different way to the other railway companies in Britain because it adopted regional divisions, each with its own general manager and departmental offices, with a limited number of all-line appointments under R.L. Wedgwood as Chief General Manager at Kings Cross. The system worked well and the transition was smooth. The LNER was efficient and people knew exactly where they stood with it, as this warning to trespassers emphasises.

The first passenger coach, *Experiment*, had longitudinal seats, no springs and was very uncomfortable. However, within a few years coach design had advanced somewhat. This example in Darlington's North Road Railway Museum, has first- and second-class compartments, side-to-side seating – if you sit with your back to the engine you don't know where you are going, but can see where you've been! – springs and an outside luggage rack. 'Tennant' locomotive 1463 is alongside it.

A bell inscribed 'S&D Railway, 1833'. At one time it was rung to mark the beginning and end of shifts on the railway.

An extension of the S&DR from riverside wharves at Bowesfield Lane, Stockton, later to become Bowesfield Junction, was opened on 27 December 1830 as part of a new development on the Yorkshire bank of the Tees, downstream at Port Darlington, later to become Middlesbrough. In 1913, following a feasibility study in the USA by Sir Vincent Raven, Chief Mechanical Engineer of the NER, and Charles Merz, a leading name in the electrical world, the Shildon–Newport, Middlesbrough route was chosen for a pilot scheme for railway electrification which, if successful, would provide the spur for Sir Vincent Raven's ultimate objective of main line electrification between York and Newcastle. Work started on the electric infrastructure on 16 June 1913. In about 1915, electric locomotive No. 3, the first electric goods engine, was making trial runs along the Shildon to Newport route. Here it is seen alongside an NER class P2 0–6–0 goods engine – strange (track) bed fellows! The years of depression during the 1920s and 1930s had a detrimental effect on railway freight and in 1935 electrification, no longer a commercially viable proposition, was abandoned.

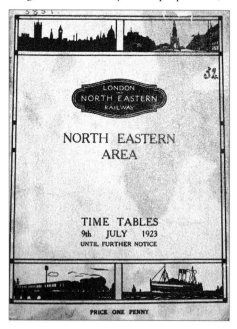

Steam retains pride of place on both land and at sea in the illustrations decorating this 1923 LNER timetable.

CHAPTER TWO

DARLINGTON RAILWAY WORKSHOPS

The first locomotive to be built in the North Road shops, Darlington, Contractor 0–6–0.
The year was 1864.

Ninety-three years later, in October 1957, No. 84029 was the last steam locomotive to be built at the North Road shops, Darlington.

In 1901, when this photograph was taken, this was the oldest working locomotive in the world. It is George Stephenson's *Hetton Colliery* locomotive, which was built in 1822. In the S&DR celebrations of 1925 it headed a cavalcade from Shildon to Stockton and passed the grandstand filled with dignitaries that included the Duke and Duchess of York, later King George VI and Queen Elizabeth, LNER directors Viscount Grey of Falloden and Sir Hugh Bell, Lady Bell and the company's Chief General Manager, Sir Ralph Wedgwood. The *Northern Echo* of 3 July 1925 reported the centenary parade and also detailed a proposal to cut the pay of railway staff by 5 per cent as a result of financial difficulties.

The boys at the back of this group, photographed at North Road Railway Works just before the outbreak of the First World War, are fourteen years old and in their first job. There was no shortage of work at that time.

A new engine being made at North Road Railway Workshops.

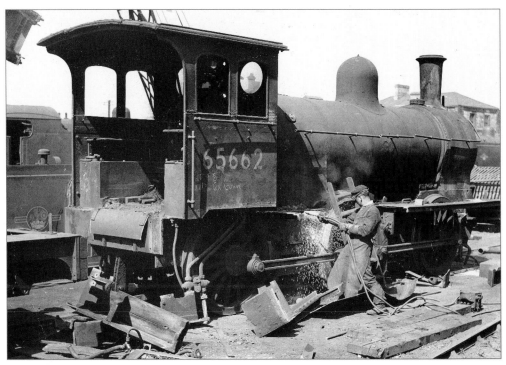

Darlington's scrap depot where all the steam engines are demolished. This photograph was taken in 1960 when the North Road Railway Workshop itself was facing the same fate.

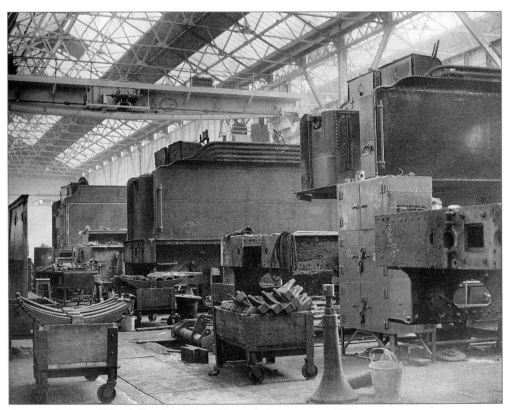

A general view of North Road Works with work in progress, 1930s.

An overview of the North Road Works, October 1964. The designs are more advanced and the locomotives larger.

Skilled tradesman Frank Thompson, October 1965. He is justifiably proud of his role as part of a locomotive construction team, and it shows! The North Road Railway Workshops employed a highly skilled workforce, renowned for its high standards of workmanship and the reliability of the steam engines it produced.

The trade of blacksmith is essential to locomotive construction. Here Don Robson demonstrates his skill at the forge, 1 October 1965.

'Will I get a job here when I'm old enough?' A contemplative urchin in wrinkled stockings sits on a brick column that supports railings under the railway works' clock. Only time will tell; but it is 1964 and time is running out.

Ken Watson, Arnold Griffiths and Jimmy Clarke stand on an engine they are helping to build, 1947.

A mass protest march against unemployment took place at the North Road shops in September 1962.

A time for relaxation and for helping a good cause, the North Road shops' carnival, 20 September 1962.

The locomotive works manager's invitation to staff to attend the annual dinner and dance, 7 February 1964.

North Road Railway Workshops finished for the day, 20 September 1962.

North Road Railway Workshops finished for good, 2 April 1966.

North Road Railway Workshops, *c.* 1964. 'See those engines, son? They represent the best of Durham steam; and we built them here in Darlington, me and my mates.'

'See that cat, son? She was on the staff as a mouser. Remember those steam engines I showed you? We built them right here in this workshop. Now it's all over. The good days are gone. This is all that's left: and empty space and our mouser. Wonder who'll feed her now? Give her a saucer of milk? It looks forlorn doesn't it? But some of the past remains. Lots of the steam locos we built are still around. And while they are there, so is our pride.'

CHAPTER THREE

D&BCR AND SD&LUR LINES

DARLINGTON & BARNARD CASTLE RAILWAY.

Time Table from JULY 9th, 1856.

Going West.				Going East.			
	1	**2**	**3**		**1**	**2**	**2**
LEAVE	1 2 3 / a.m.	1 2 / p.m.	1 2 / p.m.	LEAVE	1 2 3 / a.m.	1 2 / p.m.	1 2 / p.m.
Darlington	7 30	12 10	4 45	Barnard Castle ...	9 0	1 10	5 45
Piercebridge ...	7 45	12 25	5 0	Winston for Staindrop	9 15	1 25	6 0
Gainford	7 53	12 33	5 8	Gainford ...	9 23	1 33	6 8
Winston for Staindrop	8 0	12 40	5 15	Piercebridge ...	9 30	1 40	6 15
Barnard Castle *arrive*	8 15	12 55	5 30	Darlington *arrive*	9 45	1 55	6 25

YORK AND NEWCASTLE TRAINS.							
Trains leave Darlington for York ...	7 15	9 57	1 5	2 25	6 0	8 19	12 30
" " Newcastle	4 52	8 0	10 18	1 50	3 50	5 55	8 7

RETURN TICKETS

Will be issued from Barnard Castle to REDCAR on TUESDAYS and FRIDAYS, by No. 1 going East, to return the same day.—Also on Saturdays to return on MONDAYS.—Fares there and back, 1st Class, 7s. 6d : 2nd Class, 5s. 6d.

From Darlington, Bishop Auckland, Stockton, Middlesbro', and Redcar, to Barnard Castle, on Wednesdays, by Nos. 1 and 2.

From Barnard Castle to Darlington on Mondays, and Stockton on Wednesdays, by No. 1 Train.

On SUNDAYS the Mail Train only will run, viz., from Darlington at 7·30, and return from Barnard Castle at 5·45, calling at the intermediate Stations.

Merchandise Trains will run daily, (except Sundays) after Wednesday the 9th, leaving Darlington at 2 p.m., and Barnard Castle at 6 p.m.

Darlington, July, 1856.

HARRISON PENNEY, PRINTER, DARLINGTON.

This is the very first timetable for the Darlington to Barnard Castle Railway and details passenger-train movements from 9 July 1856. Authorised by an Act of Parliament of 1854, the line was opened a day earlier on 8 July 1856. The railway terminated at Barnard Castle in what was to become, following the line's extension, the goods depot. In 1859 the S&DR took over and, in turn, was absorbed by the NER in 1863.

STOCKTON AND DARLINGTON RAILWAY COMPANY.

SOUTH DURHAM LINE,

TO TEBAY AND THE LAKE DISTRICT.

Time Table for September, 1861.

Going West.		1 2 3 a.m.	1 2 a.m. 10 30	Wednesdays only p.m.	Going East.		Wednesdays only	1 2 3 a.m. 10 15	1 2 p.m. 4 0
REDCAR	Depart				TEBAY	Depart		10 15	4 0
MIDDLESBRO'	"	6 0	12 10		GAISGILL	"		10 20	4 10
STOCKTON	"	6 10	12 20		NEWBIGGEN	"		10 30	4 16
DARLINGTON	"	7 0	1 0		KIRBY STEPHEN	"	7 40	10 50	4 35
BARNARD CASTLE	"	7 10	1 40	2 50	BARRAS	"			
LARTINGTON	"	7 45	1 45	3 0	BOWES	"	8 35	11 35	5 15
BOWES	"	7 55	1 55	3 15	LARTINGTON	"	8 40	11 40	5 20
BARRAS	"				BARNARD CASTLE	"	8 50	12 0	5 40
KIRBY STEPHEN	"	8 45	2 45	4 10	DARLINGTON	"		1 40	6 35
NEWBIGGEN	"	9 0	3 0		STOCKTON	"		2 15	7 5
GAISGILL	"	9 7	3 7		MIDDLESBRO'	"		2 23	7 55
TEBAY	Arrive	9 15	3 15		REDCAR	Arrive		3 0	7 45

TIME TABLE SHOWING THE CONNEXION WITH TRAINS NORTH AND SOUTH FROM TEBAY.

	a.m.	p.m.
Trains from Tebay to Penrith and the North	9 30	5 29
Ditto .... Lancaster and the South	9 31	5 39

Tourists Tickets will be issued from the Principal Stations on the Stockton and Darlington Railway to Tebay, available for return on any day within a month from the date of issue.

HARRISON, PENNEY, PRINTER, PREBEND ROW & PRIESTGATE, DARLINGTON.

A timetable of a century ago before the Eden Valley line was opened.

direction with an extra train on market days.

Excursion trains to the Lake District soon began. The first left Darlington for Windermere three weeks after the opening. It carried 21 first class passengers, who paid 7s 6d, and 154 second class, who paid 4s return. Unfortunately, on the way back the engine Fox was derailed, the driver killed and several passengers injured.

The Royal Assent for the Eden Valley line, was given on May 31, 1858, and the first sod cut at Appleby on August 4. There was the usual procession with 16 banners, three of which were "May Westmorland Flourish," "Peace and Plenty," and "Civil and Religious Liberty." The lunch, at the King's Head, was followed by 15 toasts.

On these railways from Barnard Castle to Tebay and Penrith, local traffic has always been very light. They have been sustained by the traffic from County Durham to Barrow and West Cumberland and back.

Probably no English railway of similar size has served so wide an area and left it so little changed. No large towns have grown up on the route, and the villages and small towns have retained their character.

The building of the railways was a personal triumph for Thomas Bouch and greatly enhanced his reputation. Among many railways for which he later acted as engineer was the Cockermouth, Keswick and Penrith.

For bridging the Tay he was knighted by Queen Victoria. But the collapse of the Tay Bridge in a storm in 1879, while an engine, five coaches and 75 passengers were crossing it, brought about his professional disgrace. He died the following year.

After the Tay disaster, the Board of Trade ordered an examination of the Belah, Deepdale and Tees viaducts. But T. E. Harrison, engineer to the North-Eastern Railway, was satisfied with them, and they still stand as Bouch's worthy memorial.

On 7 August 1861, the extension westwards over the Pennines at Stainmore summit from Barnard Castle to Tebay was opened as the South Durham and Lancashire Union Railway. This S&DR timetable for September 1861 details the north and south main line connections from Tebay.

Emblem of the South Durham & Lancashire Union Railway Company.

Emblem of the Eden Valley Railway Company.

The main reason for building the South Durham and Lancashire Union Railway was to haul Durham coke to the blast furnaces around Barrow-in-Furness in West Cumberland, and furnace ore to Cleveland by a more direct route than the circuitous one via Newcastle and Carlisle then in use. The line, with its spectacular viaducts, climbed steadily westwards from Barnard Castle over the bleak Pennines, crossed Stainmore summit at 1,370 ft, descended the steep escarpment to Kirkby Stephen in the Eden Valley and continued via Tebay to the Cumberland furnaces. Acts for the construction of the South Durham and Lancashire Union and the Eden Valley Railways of 1857 and 1858 paved the way for a century of railway communication between the industrial north-east of England and Cumberland and Westmorland. The elegant viaduct over the River Tees, near Barnard Castle, on the day the line was opened for traffic, 7 August 1861, is seen here. The viaduct has now been demolished.

Two of the viaducts along the Stainmore line, Belah and Deepdale, were of lattice construction and designed by Thomas Bouch. Here, Deepdale is being demolished in 1964.

41

J21 locomotive 0–6–0 No. 65033 departs from Darlington on its last run over Stainmore summit, 7 May 1960.

J21 class 0–6–0 No. 65033 in full steam during its last run, 7 May 1960.

CHAPTER FOUR

THE WEAR VALLEY LINE

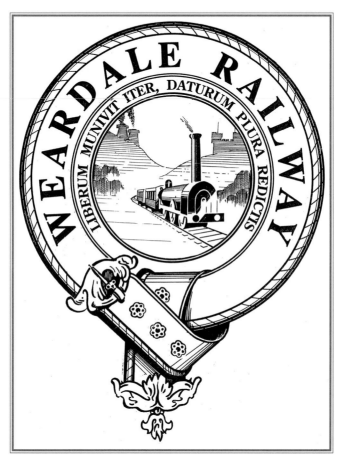

The emblem of the Weardale Railway.

Members of the Darlington and NE branch of the Railway Correspondents and Travel Society who travelled on the last goods train between St John's Chapel and Wearhead. They are seen on the train as it leaves Bishop Auckland on 31 December 1960. The branch secretary, K. Cockrill, is holding the vertical rail.

This picture, taken in January 1983, shows the full length of a Settle and Carlisle special being hauled by LNER class K1 2–6–0 No. 2005. The locomotive was in regular use on the Weardale line.

The Wear Valley line follows the banks of the River Wear. Here an 'Enthusiastic Special', hauled by LNER Gresley-designed class K4 No. 3442 *The Great Marquess*. Built in Darlington in 1937, it heads towards Witton-le-Wear in 1964.

Although an independent line, the Wear Valley Railway was operated by the S&DR. Authorised under an Act of Parliament of 1845, the line was opened as far as Wolsingham, seen here, on 3 August 1847. The extension to Stanhope was completed in 1852. The Wear Valley Railway was purchased by the S&DR in 1858 and became part of the NER in 1863. Wolsingham, with its Gothic booking hall and station house, is now a private dwelling.

On the 0910 Bishop Auckland to St John's Chapel goods, J26 0–6–0 No. 65735, busies itself shunting at Stanhope on 4 May 1962. The area is now overgrown by vegetation.

The Wear Valley Extension Railway, formed in 1892 and taken over by the NER in 1894, continued the line to Wearhead. It opened on 21 October 1895, much of its revenue created by stone traffic from the quarries *en route*. On 2 January 1961, all traffic ceased between St John's Chapel and Wearhead and from 1 November 1965 all freight services terminated at Westgate. The line from Westgate to Eastgate closed on 1 July 1968. Between then and 10 April 1993 the line between Bishop Auckland and Eastgate, with its cement works, remained open. Following its closure, a preservation society for the Wear Valley line was formed. Here a supporting cheque is being presented by William McAlpine to Harry Russell, Wear Valley District Council Mayor, at Stanhope station during a visit by the Minister of State for Public Transport, Roger Freeman, 10 January 1994.

Renewing sleepers on the Wear Valley Railway line just beyond Stanhope, 18 July 1963. Passenger trains no longer used the track but it was still maintained for goods traffic. The repair gang comprised, left to right, Mr N. Harrison of Stanhope, Mr W.L. Bee of St John's Chapel, Mr F. Jopling of Stanhope, and Mr A. Allison of Westgate.

Ex-LNER class J39 0–6–0 No. 64927, a freight locomotive, shunts mineral wagons in Eastgate station, *c.* 1960.

View from the footplate of J26 0–6–0 No. 65735 as it plods along from Westgate-in-Weardale to St John's Chapel, 4 May 1962.

B1 4–6–0 No. 61037 *Jairou* at St John's Chapel with the Railway Correspondents and Travel Society/Stephenson Locomotive Society North Eastern Tour returning to Bishop Auckland, 28 September 1963.

CHAPTER FIVE

SHILDON WORKS

The S&DR Company established Shildon Works in 1833 to maintain and build locomotives. The present works, seen here, was built close to the site from which the first steam-hauled passenger train began its journey to Stockton in 1825. From the late 1860s, Shildon Works had a major responsibility for building and maintaining freight rolling stock, many vehicles of new design having been proved and manufactured there. The works, which occupied 55 acres, including 13 acres of covered workshops, employed, at their peak, a workforce of approximately 2,600. Shildon Works closed in about 1983 and many of the workshops are now occupied by private firms.

On 3 December 1980, Shildon Works handed over its 10,000th 'Merry-Go-Round' coal wagon to British Rail. Since its introduction on a trial basis in 1964, the 'Merry-Go-Round' became a widespread service that efficiently moved some 45 per cent of all the fuel used by the Central Electricity Board. Here a high-capacity 'Merry-Go-Round' wagon is being lowered and guided into position on the under-frame on 21 August 1976.

Apprentices at Shildon Works, *c.* 1920.

Apprentice fitters Ian Jackson and Peter Bennet at work on the replica of Timothy Hackworth's *Sans Pareil* ('Without Equal') at Shildon Works before the locomotive and tender were painted in readiness for the 150th anniversary of the Liverpool and Manchester Railway in May 1980. The forgings, fabrications and machining were done at Shildon.

The single line near Shildon tunnel, bottom left. The double track was reduced to single because of concern that the swaying of passing carriages might cause an accident.

Henry Oakley GNR class U 4–4–2 No. 990, once the pride of British railways, in Shildon, 22 August 1975. It was the first 'Atlantic' type locomotive and once regularly hauled the 'Flying Scotsman'. Behind it is *Patrick Stirling* class, 'Stirling Single' 4–4–2 No. 1, which was introduced in 1870 to Patrick Stirling's design. This elegant passenger class was built until 1895. Its driving wheels were 8 ft in diameter, hence its name, 'Stirling Eight Footer'.

LNER class K1 2–6–0 No. 2005 pulling 'The North Eastern' out of Darlington destined for Shildon, early 1984.

CHAPTER SIX

MORE SOUTH WEST DURHAM STEAM

Built in 1845 for the S&DR, Derwent *was presented to the North Eastern Railway in 1898 by Pease and Partners.*

Derwent was designed and built by Alfred Kitchen, son of the founder of Whessoe. Whessoe, once Darlington's largest employer, originated in 1790. Throughout its 200 year history, Whessoe has manufactured almost every type of engineering product from small castings for the S&DR to nuclear power stations. When a plaque was made for the front of the *Derwent*, no mention was made of Alfred Kitchen. The omission was rectified on 16 January 1969 when Mr Douglas Lindley, publicity officer for Whessoe, left, handed over this new plaque to Mr Scholes, curator of historical relics for British Rail, right. Mr G.C. Renton, station master of Darlington Bank Top, is in the middle.

This shot of LNER class V2 *Green Arrow* 2–6–2 No. 4771 pulling 'The North Eastern' was taken on 21 July 1986. Almost a year later, on 11 July 1987, this magnificent locomotive in its LNER livery of apple green was at Darlington Bank Top station pulling the Darlington Bank Top Station Centenary Express. Five of this class of locomotive were built in 1936 as the forerunners of a new class designed to meet the ever-increasing demands for fast and reliable mixed traffic locomotives. At the outbreak of the Second World War, almost 100 of these locomotives were in service and more were built until 1944. V2s could work as well as the larger 'Pacific' locomotives. The last time the *Green Arrow* was in steam was on 5 September 1992. The driver was Rodney Lyttom. This locomotive has now been fully restored to BR livery. It is now No. 60800.

A special railtour train from Nottingham Victoria arrives at the north end of platform 4, Bank Top station, Darlington, 12 May 1962. Headed by Southern Region 'Schools' class *Cheltenham* 4–4–0, No. 30925 and, behind it, ex-LMS class 2P *The East Midlander* 4–4–0 No. 40646.

LNER class A2 *Blue Peter* 4–6–2 No. 60532 and the support coach of 'The Heart of Midlothian' pictured, broken down, in Darlington station. The name *Blue Peter* is derived from two sources: the International Code Flag 'P' used by vessels about to leave port, and the 1939 winner of the Derby, the 2,000 Guineas and other races owned by Lord Rosebery. The horse, Blue Peter, earned Lord Rosebery almost £32,000, enough to buy three Doncaster 'Pacific' locomotives at that time. A2 class locomotives often worked expresses on the coast route between Northallerton and Newcastle via Stockton and Hartlepool.

If the television goes 'wonky', slap it: if the vacuum cleaner won't work, kick it: if the gate collapses, use binder twine. All these methods seem to work, but there are limits. Trying to fix *Blue Peter*'s driving rod with cord is the height of optimism; nothing to smile about: in fact it makes you feel blue.

LNER class A4 *Sir Nigel Gresley* 4–6–2 No. 60007, the 'Tyne-Tees Pullman', at Darlington's Bank Top station, 11 June 1995.

LMS 'Princess Royal' class *Duchess of Hamilton* 4–6–2 No. 46229, pulling the 'Northern Belle' at Eaglescliffe, 18 March 1985.

LNER class A4 *Sir Nigel Gresley* 4–6–2 No. 60007, pulling the 'Tyne-Tees Pullman', setting out from Darlington's Bank Top station on a nostalgic trip to London's Kings Cross loaded with steam-train enthusiasts, 11 June 1995. No. 60007 was the 100th 'Pacific' locomotive built for the LNER to Mr Gresley's design. The A4s were a development of the A3 class and thirty-five of them were designed and built specifically to haul the fast non-stop trains between Kings Cross and all the northern cities on the LNER system. In recognition of his ability as a locomotive designer and engineer, Mr Gresley was knighted in 1937, hence the locomotive's name.

LNER K4 class *The Great Marquess* 2–6–0 No. 3442, pulling an Ian Allan railtour in 1964, is standing on the line at North Road station, Darlington, now occupied by the town's railway museum. *The Great Marquess* was built in Darlington for the West Highland run in Scotland. It was saved from the scrap heap by a wealthy Yorkshire carpet manufacturer, Lord David Garnock of Shipley, who had admired it from boyhood; he purchased it from British Rail and brought it back to Darlington on 5 October 1964.

The last train from Darlington to Crook, pulled by LMS class 4MT locomotive 2–6–0 No. 43106 in 1965 at Bishop Auckland station, now demolished.

Class A4 locomotives were the pride of the LNER. This impressive example of an LNER class A4 locomotive *William Whitelaw* 4–6–2 No. 60004, is steaming under some notable NER signal gantries at Bishop Auckland with a special train in 1965.

It was through the *Northern Echo* that railway employees at the little railway station in the centre of Crook learned of the line's closure. The 100-year-old station had a staff of 10: a station master, 2 porters, 3 clerks and 4 signalmen. Mr John Marsh of Shildon, a station relief clerk, said, 'Everybody here has been expecting it. We all believe this is one of the sillier ways to try and cut costs on British Railways. This is one of the most lucrative stations on the line. Trains leaving here in the morning and coming back at night are packed full. I don't think you can really lay the blame at the feet of anyone in particular, whether it be Marples or Dr Beeching. All you can say is that this seems to be a general policy of the railways. It works like this. First they take off the best trains and give the public a poorer train service which, of course, they do not patronise. Then they turn round and say that no one is using it and so the line has to go. That is what happened when the Durham line went.'

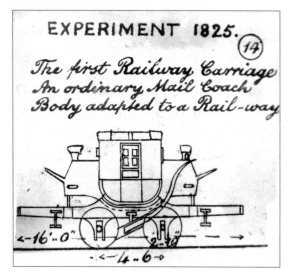

EXPERIMENT 1825.

(14)

The first Railway Carriage An ordinary Mail Coach Body adapted to a Rail-way

When the S&DR line opened officially on 27 September 1825, among the wagons hauled to Stockton was *Experiment*, the very first passenger coach. From this small beginning today's sophisticated railway coaches have developed. Similarly, the opening of the S&DR set the pattern for the development of railways throughout the world with branch lines linking centres of population and special stations being built to handle freight and passenger traffic. Some of the oldest branch lines in England are in County Durham. In the south-west of the county, coal, in particular, and agricultural traffic were the two main industries on which the lines depended. The following branch lines, together with those already mentioned, covered most of south-west Durham before the Beeching cuts when steam ruled supreme. The 34-mile-long Darlington Bank Top to Blackhill line was built to convey coal from collieries around Witton Park to the River Tees. Until 1833, when the S&DR introduced regular steam trains for passengers, they were carried by horse-drawn coaches. The S&DR section was opened on 27 September 1825, the extension to Bishop Auckland was opened to passengers on 8 November 1843, the extension from Crook to Waskerley on 1 September 1845, and the section from Burnhill Junction to Whitehall Junction on 4 July 1859 providing a through service along this route from Darlington to Blackhill. A 5-mile-long line southwards from Forcett was opened for mineral traffic in October 1866. It was worked by the NER, became part of the LNER in 1923 and was closed by British Railways on 2 November 1964. The Merrybent and Darlington Railway opened for mineral traffic on 1 June 1870 to serve quarries at Barlow. The NER took over this 6½-mile-long line in 1890. It closed on 6 July 1950. The Tees Valley Railway, an 8¾-mile-long branch from Barnard Castle to Middleton-in-Teesdale conveyed lead and stone from Upper Teesdale. It was opened to passenger traffic on 12 May 1863 and this service was closed on 30 November 1964; it closed to freight on 5 April 1965. Opened to passenger traffic on 1 August 1863, part of this 15-mile-long line from West Auckland was built over the S&DR Butterknowle goods branch, which BR closed on 30 September 1963. Passenger services were withdrawn on 12 June and freight on 18 June 1962. Known as the Byers Green branch, the 9½-mile-long line from Bishop Auckland to Ferryhill was opened on 31 March 1837 to carry coals to the coast, despite objections from local landowners. A passenger service was started in 1845 and ceased in 1867, but was restarted on 1 June 1878. That section of the line from Bishop Auckland to Spennymoor ceased on 4 December 1939. BR withdrew the passenger service from Spennymoor to Stockton via Ferryhill on 31 March 1952. The Newcastle and Darlington Junction (Durham branches) Act of 1846 authorised the 11-mile-long Bishop Auckland to Durham line, which opened on 1 April 1857. The NER passenger service provided ten passenger trains per weekday and two on Sundays. The passenger service ceased on 4 May 1964, while the freight service ceased on 5 August 1968.

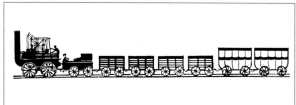

Locomotion hauling chaldrons and passenger coaches.

CHAPTER SEVEN

THE TANFIELD RAILWAY

The Tanfield Railway is built on a 3-mile section of the original Tanfield wagonway between Sunniside and Marley Hill. The Tanfield wagonway is the most famous of Tyneside's early wooden railways. It opened as early as 1725 to serve the local coal industry and was an advanced engineering enterprise, a worthy forerunner of the nineteenth-century steam railways. The wagonway's most famous features were an embankment 100 ft high and the Causey Arch, seen here. Built by Ralph Wood in 1727, it was the largest single-span bridge in Britain, and remained so for the next thirty years. Because no one had ever built such a bridge before, Ralph Wood had to rely on Roman technology.

The original Tanfield wagonways were of the wooden flanged type. These were replaced by iron ones in 1839 and it was on the type of iron flanged rail seen here that Hedley's engine ran before it was supplied with flanged wheels. The building of the Tanfield wagonway was probably the first major engineering feat of the Industrial Revolution in Britain. An original wagon stands on a short section of track close to Causey Arch to remind us of those days, 300 years ago.

William Hedley, one time engineer at Wylam Colliery, and later its viewer (manager), was one of many locomotive engineers who inspired George Stephenson. By 1813 he had successfully built a smooth-wheeled engine that ran for many years on the colliery's cast-iron rails, which replaced wooden ones. Two of Hedley's later engines, dating from 1828 and 1832, were called *Puffing Billy* and *Wylam Dilly*, two of the earliest locomotives still in existence. The original wagons were powered by horses and this is an example of the type of lantern used on the horse-drawn wagons.

The Tanfield line is run by enthusiasts who are not above enlisting the help of other like-minded people. Here, in July 1992, the Bishop of Durham helps youngsters on a restoration job at the railway. That's the spirit – the shovel practice could come in handy if, when your time comes, St Peter won't let you in!

At Tanfield's annual steam gala on 1 September 1987 over 1,000 steam lovers could, for the first time, watch coal-fired trains using the newly restored stretch of line. The engine seen here is *Sir Cecil A. Cochrane* No. 7409 0–4–0, a saddle tank built by Robert Stephenson and Hawthorn in 1948.

When the Tanfield Railway was built it was essential that the industrial character of the wagonway was preserved; but, of course, the new line is for carrying passengers. Particularly noteworthy in this picture are saloon coaches one and four. At first sight these balcony end four-wheelers look like the coaches supplied at the turn of the century to pioneer British Light Railways like the Lambourn and Rother Valley. This is intentional as the Tanfield line is very close in spirit to this earlier generation of minor railways and the saloon coaches have been built by the Tanfield volunteers to create an authentic atmosphere.

Tanfield is the home of one of the best collections of industrial steam locomotives in the country, most of them having been built locally on Tyneside. The oldest is *Black Hawthorn* 0–4–0, a saddle tank, Wellington engine, built in 1873. There is also a Robert Stephenson and Hawthorn, 0–4–0, saddle tank of 1884 vintage. More typical are the Hawthorn Leslies and Robert Stephenson and Hawthorn 4 and 6 coupled saddle tanks, of which the newest example was built in 1951. There are four Andrew Barclay locomotives, of which perhaps the best known is 0–6–0 side tank No. 17, a long-time favourite from the Waterside Colliery in Ayrshire. *Irwell*, seen here, No. 1672 0–4–0 saddle tank was built by Hudswell Clarke of Leeds in 1937.

Andrew Contin and Andrew Knott, two enthusiasts, standing in front of two saddle tanks in steam. The NCB locomotive on the left, No. 38, was built by Robert Stephenson and Hawthorn in 1954.

On 11 April 1984, striking miners failed to dampen the resourcefulness of Eric Maxwell, an industrial chemist, and Derek Charlton, a company representative, as they prepared to carry out some steam tests. They simply collected scrap wood for firing the locomotives. Here, from the front, Richard Charlton, Derek Charlton, Stewart Waugh and George Ridley are setting up steam. 'In the late sixties,' said Eric, 'we found ourselves restoring engines only to see them go down south. That galled us and we decided to do something about it, and we were operating on a small scale in 1971. This area is steeped in railway history, yet few people know of it. We want people to take pride in local engines and the very early role Tyneside played in the railways. We have a story to tell and a passion for steam engines.'

A special treat for Aidan Spencer as he sets off the steam trains with the help of Bill Hampson on 28 August 1984, during a two-day steam event at Tanfield.

No. 49 0–4–0, a saddle tank built by Robert Stephenson and Hawthorn, has a smile on its face at Tanfield Railway Children's weekend, August 1984. It has the face of Thomas the Tank Engine but is not called this for copyright reasons.

CHAPTER EIGHT

STANHOPE TO SOUTH SHIELDS

It was Weardale's mineral wealth that attracted the railway promoters and the Stanhope and Tyne Railway Company, floated in 1832, led the way. The full length of the line was opened on 10 September 1834 and, because it was not authorised by an Act of Parliament, expensive wayleaves had to be paid to cross the countryside. The railway, which included several cable-worked inclines, climbed steeply from Stanhope to its summit of 1,474 ft at Parkend.
Rookhope, lying snugly in the bottom of a valley some 4 miles north-west of Stanhope, became a lead mining centre in the early nineteenth century because the richest yields in Weardale were found there. The Weardale Iron Co., formed in 1846, depended on Weardale for all its limestone and much of its iron ore. It approached the Stanhope and Derwent Railway for a line to be built across the moors from Parkhead to Rookhope, Boltshope and Stanhope. The request was refused, so the Weardale Iron Co. built its own railway to reach the ore deposits. The first part of this system became known as the Weatherhill and Rookhope Railway. The line left Rookhope up a 2,000-yd long incline with a gradient that eased from 1 in 6 at its foot to 1 in 12 at its top. It then curved east, contouring around Stanhope Common. At its highest point the line is 1,679 ft above sea level, which gives it the distinction of having been the highest standard gauge line ever built on mainland Britain. The line closed in 1923. The limestone from the Crawley Side quarries at Stanhope was hauled up gradients so steep it is amazing that the line was ever built. This view of Hog Hill tunnel, in about 1913, on the Crawley incline is looking south, down it, showing the interlaced track.

Crawley engine house, looking north, early 1900s. All traffic leaving or entering Crawley Side had to be rope-hauled up and down the incline by the Crawley standing engine inside this engine house, sited at the incline's top. The western terminus of the S&TR was at the foot of Crawley incline, which midway down split into two spurs, one to Ashes Quarry and one to Crawley Side lime kilns. The S&TR projected the route down the Crawley incline to enable lime from Crawley Side Kilns, which they owned, to be carried to the many depots they had at strategic points all the way to South Shields.

Weatherhill incline top, 31 July 1938. This notorious line, which closed on 28 April 1951, was built to carry limestone and coal from Medomsley. The Weatherhill incline climbs for 1 mile and 128 yd to the engine house at its top. Some of the gradients are as steep as 1 in 12 and, when operative, the incline was worked on the three-rail principle with a passing loop. Wagons were raised or lowered in sets of four or six. But before this could be effected, the ropes of the Crawley standing engine had to be exchanged for the much longer rope of the Weatherhill standing engine.

Q6 0–8–0 No. 63372 at Weatherhill, *c.* 1957. Robert Stephenson was the line's consultant engineer and its motive power was mixed: 14½ miles being by stationary engines, 14½ miles by horse and ¾ of a mile by gravity. It is surprising that, considering the problems encountered using horses, standing engines and gradients which were so steep that at first they prevented the use of locomotives, the line was ever built. Locomotives were not used on it until after 1845, and then only on short sections.

K1 2–6–0 No. 62027 at Waskerley, 28 September 1963. In 1842, when the Stanhope and Tyne Railway became insolvent, the section from Consett to Stanhope, which included Waskerley, was sold to the Derwent Iron Co. The other end of the line became the Pontop and South Shields Railway, which, in 1847, became part of the York, Newcastle and Berwick Railway and was then acquired by the NER in 1854. The S&DR took over the Derwent Iron Co. in 1845 and it became part of the NER in 1863.

Snow clearing along the Waskerley line was very important because around this increasingly important station a railway township had been created. There were rows of back-to-back stone and slate cottages, a chapel, shops, a club and a school, but no pub. In this isolated moorland community several hundred people lived, worked and played in the boom years of the second half of the nineteenth century.

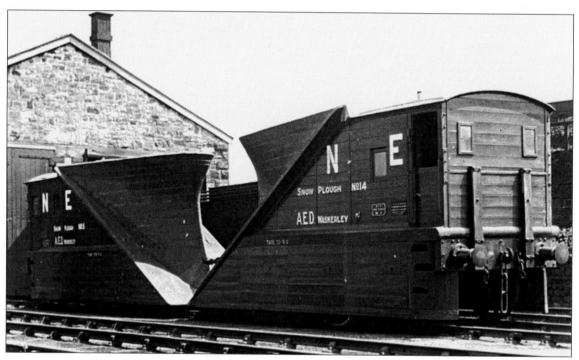

If ever a station needed snow ploughs, Waskerley did. For many railwaymen Waskerley was an arduous but necessary step on the promotion ladder. Living conditions were spartan, the weather usually foul and the surroundings bleak. Living there separated the sheep from the goats, yet working on the highest passenger line in England, despite its many drawbacks, frequently bred people of sterling character.

Standing outside Waskerley wagon shop is NER class B 0–6–0 No. 1105, built at Darlington in 1889 and rebuilt to class No. 8 by the LNER.

Once over the summit at Weatherhill, the line provided several long sidings, then crossed bleak moorland as single track contouring at 1,400 ft for ¾ of a mile, then descending at 1 in 80 to Parkhead wheelhouse. The whole of this section was originally worked by horses. For a further mile eastwards from the Parkhead wheelhouse to the Meeting Slacks wheelhouse a main and tail endless rope system was used on a further downhill gradient, which, for the most part, was 1 in 80. In 1847, a lengthy deviation was provided to the south of the original line, which completely bypassed the Parkhead wheelhouse. From then on, locomotives worked all the way from the Weatherhill engine house to the Meeting Slacks engine house. From Meeting Slacks the rope was attached for a further 1 mile 453 yd to Waskerley on gradients from 1 in 47 to 1 in 35. Waskerley, sited on the short stretch of level ground at the foot of the Meeting Slacks incline, assumed real importance after 1845 when the Weardale extension came up from the south. This view of almost featureless moorland is from Waskerley's derelict coal stage; C shed would have been situated in the foreground.

The line continued north-east from Waskerley downhill to Nanny Mayor's self-acting incline, which was almost ⅔ of a mile long with gradients of between 1 in 10 and 1 in 13. It was capable of dealing with eight wagons each way and Mr Mayor kept a lineside alehouse at the foot of the incline. From the foot of the incline to 3½ miles distant Hownes Gill, the next obstacle, the grades were gentle and horse-drawn 'dandy' carts were used along it. Nanny Mayor's incline closed on 4 July 1859. Another line continued eastwards from Waskerley. It soon swung south to Burn Hill Junction from where a gentler graded line went north to rejoin the original line down Nanny Mayor's incline, which it was built to supersede, at Whitehall. This view of Nanny Mayor's incline from Waskerley was taken on 26 September 1957 and the new line can be seen on the right.

Rowley station, near Hownes Gill, viewed from the last Darlington to Blackhill train, 21 May 1939. The station was demolished brick by brick in 1972 and rebuilt at nearby Beamish Museum in 1976, where it remains today.

Because of the parlous state of the Stanhope and Tyne Railway finances, the company was not initially able to build a viaduct across the precipitous dry gorge at Hownes Gill. They made do with a cliff cradle arrangement in which wagons were lowered one at a time for some 147 yd on a gradient of 1 in 2½. At the bottom, turntables enabled the wagons to be pushed off the cradle for a few yards to be repositioned in the opposite ascending cradle to be hauled up a gradient of 1 in 3, then shunted off to await assembly of the other trucks in the train. This was by far the biggest bottleneck along the line. Later, a system using funicular railways on each side hauled three trucks at a time, but it was little better than the original system. It was not until 1858 when the line's third owner built the 150-ft high Hownes Gill viaduct that the bottleneck was finally cleared. Thomas Bouch, the man who built Belah viaduct and the first Tay Bridge, built Hownes Gill viaduct, which still stands today. It contains 2½ million bricks.

K1 class 2–6–0, No. 62025 pulling the last passenger train of the Newcastle to Blackhill service and arriving at Consett, 23 May 1955.

What a way to go! The last rail service to Consett on 17 March 1984 proved a real gravy train thanks to pub landlady Margaret Hood. More than 300 enthusiasts from all over Britain packed the £10.50-a-head special on the round trip from Newcastle. Most of them sat down to a free spread in the tiny two-roomed Duke of Wellington pub, just down the street from where Consett station used to be. Helped by the ladies' darts team, Margaret spent three days preparing for the expected invasion on her three-ring, domestic cooker. Although her usual lunchtime catering is little more than a bag of cheese-and-onion crisps, on that special Saturday passengers queued outside in the snow for their quiche and curry, soup and sandwiches. But Margaret was glad she had made such an effort: 'It's cost me more than £150, but it's worth it for such an occasion. It's a dreadful shame that the lines have to go.'

The Stanhope and Tyne Railway Inn, Annfield Plain, 18 August 1959. It was renamed The Plainsman on 14 April 1981.

One of the north-east's oldest railway signal-boxes, built in about 1896, was demolished and then rebuilt brick by brick at Beamish Museum, near Stanley. It was originally sited at Rowley station.

Wagons at the top of Waskerley incline, east of Annfield Plain, 12 June 1965. On 1 January 1886, the NER built a deviation from East Castle to Annfield Plain, which was extended to Stella Gill on 13 November 1890. Passenger stations were built at Pelton, Beamish, Shield Row, Annfield Plain, Leadgate and Consett. The passenger service was introduced in 1896 from Newcastle to Blackhill via Birtley and closed on 23 May 1955. As Consett Steel Works expanded, BR ran a series of iron-ore trains from Tyne Dock to Consett. At first 01 class 2–8–0s banked by Q7 class 0–8–0s provided the motive power. Class 9F 2–10–0s replaced them, to be replaced, in turn, by class 37 diesels which were used until the Tyne Dock to Consett trains ceased to run on 5 September 1980.

From Waldridge Bank Top, looking east, down the incline, 12 June 1965.

The Stanhope and Tyne plaques pictured here at the foot of Waldridge incline are now on display at Darlington's North Road Railway Centre and Museum.

CHAPTER NINE

BLACKHILL, BEAMISH AND BOWES

Station Inspector 'Barney' Marshall, a lifelong chum of the author, gives the green light to a night express to Kings Cross, c. 1966. He is a native of Kirkby Stephen, Westmorland, as I am, and a third-generation railwayman, who started as a porter-signalman at a village station in 1948. He is seen here on the 3 a.m. shift, the one he liked best. When this picture was taken he had been Inspector for Durham station for five years. The signalmen are the only people at Durham station working through the night, with more about up to midnight than in the early hours. When working the 3 a.m. shift, 'Barney' would set his alarm for just after 2 a.m. mount his motorbike and head from his Ferryhill home to Durham in time to meet the 3.09 a.m. bringing newspapers from Manchester. A little later on the Bristol Mail would arrive on its way to Newcastle. He had to be there to see them in and as the Station Inspector it was his responsibility to signal to the guard when the train was ready to leave, and the guard, in turn, would wave his flag to the driver. Once he got the signal, the train would begin to move. 'Barney', ever confident, looks relieved to see this train move off, perhaps because the passenger looks like a Frankenstein creation!

Mr Fred Bare signals through a midnight train at Durham South signal-box, 21 November 1966. According to Mr Charles Gavin, a full-time relief signalman who travelled to twenty signal-boxes in the area at that time and could operate them all, Durham South was an easy signal-box compared to some. The levers are marked 'Up main', 'Up fast home', and with other informative words that are baffling to the uninitiated. 'Up' goes to London, 'down' to Edinburgh, 'slow' means a platform line and 'fast' the centre track. It is a complicated business, but Mr Bare, Mr Gavin and their fellow signalmen knew the system inside out for all the seventy trains that steamed through Durham during the night.

Old signals at Durham North signal-box, 24 July 1967. There have been many changes over the years from the levers and brass bells in Durham's old-style signal-boxes to the push buttons of today, which change both points and signals to set up complete routes for approaching trains. The locomotive seen here is class V3 2–6–2T No. 67688.

Authorised under an Act of Parliament of July 1855, the 6-mile long Deerness Valley Railway started as an independent line for mineral traffic only, running from Pelly Mill Junction to Waterhouses, from where it continued along an old colliery line to Billy Row. In 1858 the NER took over the working of the line and, on 1 November 1877, a passenger service was opened along it. On 1 September 1884, an intermediate station was opened at Ushaw Moor, close to the most famous of the line's wooden-trestle viaducts. The line had a direct connection with the Crook branch of the S&DR via the Stanley inclines. On 29 October 1951, BR withdrew the passenger service and on 28 October 1964, the freight service was withdrawn. Until that date, when the line closed, BR ran passenger excursions on gala days. The brick viaduct seen here, now demolished, crossed the Deerness Valley near Pelly Mill Junction.

Blackhill railway station and V3 class 2–6–2 tank No. 67658 pulling one of the last passenger trains to stop there, early in 1954. Two years after the Durham to Waterhouses branch was authorised as the independent Deerness Valley Railway in July 1855 the Pelly Mill Junction to Consett North Junction was authorised under the North Eastern Railway (Lanchester) Act of 13 July 1857. The line opened on 1 September 1862. Under an Act of Parliament of 1862 the line was extended from Blackhill to Scotswood along the Derwent Valley; it was opened on 2 December 1867. The North Eastern Railway built this branch line to prevent the North British and the London and North Western Railways from gaining access to NER and S&DR territory. The NER now had a circular service from Newcastle to Blackhill, outward via Birtley, returning via Scotswood. The passenger service from Durham to Blackhill ceased on 1 May 1939, and from Blackhill to Scotswood on 1 February 1954. The freight service from Durham to Blackhill was withdrawn on 20 June 1966, and from Blaydon to Blackhill on 11 November 1963, although no regular traffic had used that section of the branch line since 1959.

Rowlands Gill viaduct, *c.* 1900.

Rowlands Gill railway station, looking north, *c.* 1900. Beyond the road bridge on the left there are trees, but no signal-box.

Rowlands Gill railway station, looking north, 1927. Beyond the bridge there is a signal-box, but no trees.

Lampton, Hetton and Joycey Colliery locomotive No. 14 pulling a clerestory coach at Beamish Open Air Museum. The locomotive was built in 1903. Oil or gas was used for heating and lighting in this type of coach.

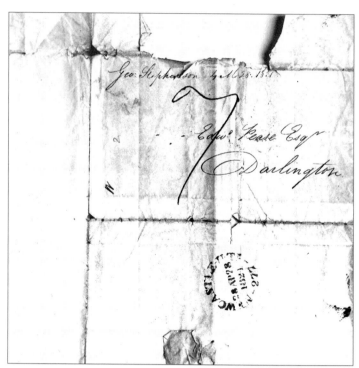

A communication from George Stephenson in Newcastle to Edward Pease in Darlington, franked on 28 April 1821.

One of the original whistles used on the Stockton and Darlington Railway.

The nameplate of the LMS class 5MT 4–6–0 No. 44767 locomotive *George Stephenson*, named after the father of the railways.

The *George Stephenson*, a locomotive with a good pedigree. It is one of 842 Stanier-designed Class 5 4–6–0 locomotives, often described as the most successful engines built by the LMS. First introduced in 1934, the original 842 were unsurpassed on either freight or express passenger duties. Soon after the Second World War, the then Chief Mechanical Engineer of the LMS, Mr H.G. Ivatt, decided that in order to keep these mixed-traffic engines abreast of modern developments a new batch of engines should be built, designed to reduce maintenance between overhauls. Of the thirty new engines built, some had 'roller bearings', at that time a new idea, and differently designed valve gears. No. 4767 was fitted with Stephenson's valve gear, a design originally introduced by George Stephenson more than a hundred years earlier. No. 4767 was the last main line locomotive in England to be fitted with outside Stephenson's valve gear. Over the years it gained a reputation for being stronger in acceleration or climbing against the grade than its sister engines. However, because the age of steam on British Rail was coming to an end, No. 4767 was withdrawn from service in 1967. It was then privately purchased as No. 44767 and during 1975 was completely overhauled and restored to its original LMS livery as No. 4767 by Ian Storey, the owner. It is fitting that this famous locomotive, which carries the Stephenson link valve gear, should have been named by the Rt Hon. William Whitelaw after the most famous of all railway engineers, George Stephenson, at the S&DR's 150th anniversary celebrations in 1975.

The Bowes Railway is a former colliery railway, laid down to carry coal from the Northumberland pits to the rivers of the north-east for shipment to London and the south-east. In mining districts large networks were owned not by the main-line companies, but by the collieries themselves. The line was originally, until 1932, called the Pontop and Jarrow Railway. The oldest section was designed by George Stephenson and ran from Mount Moor Colliery via Springwell to Jarrow. At its fullest extent the railway was 15 miles long and during its history has served as many as thirteen separate collieries. It was linked to a section of the Pelaw Main Railway in 1955, thereby including a further three mines within its orbit. Pelaw is also a stop on the former NER line between Newcastle Central and South Shields. Jarrow station is to the east on the south bank of the River Tyne. The railway had seven rope-worked inclines and three locomotive-operated sections. It was not merely concerned with the shipment of coals and for a time ran a passenger service. However, closures in the 1970s prompted conservationists and preservationists to look into the question of rescuing parts of this industrial railway. By 1974, only the section from Monkton to Jarrow was still in use, under the National Coal Board. With the closure of the line between Kibblesworth and Springwell Bank Foot, Tyne and Wear County Council considered a restoration project. In March 1976, the County Council completed the purchase of a length of track from Black Fell Bank Head, near the former Mount Moor Colliery, to Springwell Bank Head, a distance of 1¾ miles, together with the lineside buildings, winding engines and forty-one wooden wagons. This section, part of the 1826 line, consists of two inclines, 685 m at approximately 1 in 15 and 1,070 m at 1 in 70, operated by the Blackham's Hill Engine, the only preserved rope inclines in the world. This was followed in September 1977 by the purchase of the railway's engineering and wagon shops at Springwell, with much of their machinery, at the eastern end of the preserved section. The whole railway, its buildings and machinery, is now a scheduled Ancient Monument, protected by the Department of the Environment. This 0–4–0 ex-NCB saddle tank engine worked on the Bowes Railway and is now at the Bowes Railway Museum, Tyne and Wear.

CHAPTER TEN

EAST COAST BRANCHES

There were two branch lines from Durham to Sunderland: one via Murton, 14 miles long, and another, 15 miles long, via Penshaw. On 30 August 1836, a branch from Sunderland southerly to Haswell, 10 miles distant, was opened by the Durham and Sunderland Railway. A further section, from Murton to Shincliffe, near Durham, was opened on 28 June 1839. In 1893, the NER resited the Durham terminus at Elvet, closer to the city centre. At the Sunderland end of the line the original South Dock terminus was resited at Hendon in 1858, which was replaced by Central in 1879. The Durham Elvet terminus lost its regular passenger service from Pittington on 1 January 1931, but continued to be used by special trains on gala days until 1950. The freight service continued until 11 January 1954.

In April 1844, Durham Gilesgate station was opened by the Newcastle and Darlington Junction Railway. Passenger trains used it until 1857 when it was replaced by Durham's present station. Gilesgate became a goods terminus and remained so until 7 November 1966. The passenger service from Durham to Sunderland via Penshaw ceased on 4 May 1964. The line's most impressive structure is the Victoria Viaduct, which spans the River Wear. Tall and slender, with magnificent arches, its golden-coloured sandstone gleaming when bathed in sunshine, Victoria Viaduct encapsulates the very best of railway architecture. Designed by G. Walker and Burges, with T.E. Harrison as resident engineer, it was built between 1836 and 1838. Local freestone from Penshaw quarries was used to build it, while the quoins of the large arches are of Aberdeen granite. Having a height of 128 ft between rail and river levels, the main arch was said to be the largest in Europe at the time of its construction. The design was based on that of a Roman viaduct at Alcantra in Spain and it originally carried the LNER, so helping to create the first link between the Thames and the Tyne. It was one of the wonders of the early railway age and acquired its name because the last stone of the viaduct was laid on the very day of Queen Victoria's coronation. Here A4 class locomotive Sir Nigel Gresley *steams over the viaduct on the way to Edinburgh.*

Seaham Docks locomotive, built in 1873, with a vertical multi-tabular boiler, photographed in 1953.

Built in about 1876, this is probably the oldest existing industrial locomotive. It spent most of its working life at Seaham Harbour and was part of the stock of the Londonderry, Seaham and Sunderland Railway, which was owned by the Marquis of Londonderry. Apprentices at Laing Welding restored it.

Q7 class 0–8–0 No. 63460 pulls a 'North Eastern Limited' special train at Wellfield station, early 1960s. Under an Act of Parliament of 1832, a line from Hartlepool to Haswell, via Castle Eden, was opened on 23 November 1835. Then, on 30 August 1836, the Durham and Sunderland Railway opened to its terminus at Haswell; and this was later connected to the Hartlepool Railway, creating a through route between Hartlepool and Sunderland. In 1857, the NER took over the Hartlepool Railway and it remained part of the through route from Hartlepool to Sunderland until 1905 when the NER opened the coastal route via Seaham. BR withdrew the passenger service between Hartlepool and Sunderland on 9 June 1952. The line from Sunderland to Haswell closed to all traffic on 5 December 1966, and from Haswell to Hartlepool on 31 October 1978, though regular working had ceased some time earlier.

Wynyard station on the Wellfield to Stockton line, which runs north to south, at right angles to the Hartlepool to Ferryhill line, seen here in the 1950s. The Ferryhill to Hartlepool line was opened in two sections by two companies, the first, from Hartlepool to Haswell, by Hartlepool Dock and Railway Company on 23 November 1835, the remainder, from Castle Eden to Ferryhill, being opened by the Great North of England and Clarence and Hartlepool Junction Railway, the passenger service between Ferryhill and Hartlepool starting in 1846. The NER eventually took over the line, running six passenger trains, Monday to Friday, nine on Saturdays and two on Sundays. The passenger service ceased on 9 June 1952, and freight between Ferryhill and Castle Eden on 4 November 1963.

A southbound passenger train is seen crossing the Thorpe viaduct, *c*. 1950. In January 1836, the Clarence Railway opened a passenger service from Stockton to Coxhoe with the intention of extending it to Durham via Sherburn. The carriages were horse drawn and a connecting horse bus took the passengers from Coxhoe to Durham. The line was taken over by the NER and eventually passed to the LNER. Within a short time of the opening of Coxhoe Bridge station, on the Hartlepool line, the passenger service on the Stockton to Coxhoe line fell into terminal decline. On 1 March 1880, the NER opened a line from Carlton South Junction to Wellfield, making a connection with the Hartlepool to Haswell branch. There were four passenger trains daily and intermediate stations were built at Thorpe Thewles, Wynyard and Hurworth Burn. The passenger service was withdrawn by the LNER on 2 November 1931, and freight on 7 July 1966, by BR.

The Stockton to Wellfield passenger service joined the Stockton and Castle Eden branch at Redmarshall North Junction, seen here in the 1950s.

Stockton and Darlington Railway's No. 160 *Brougham*, probably the first train into Saltburn on 17 August 1861, seen here *c.* 1880.

The class K locomotive, first introduced in 1949, was a simplified development of Sir Nigel Gresley's three-cylinder K4. No. 62005 2–6–0 came into service in 1949 and spent all her working life in the north-east. She has a rare distinction among engines of having been used as a 'Royal' engine when Her Majesty the Queen visited the north of England both in 1960 and 1967, the year it was withdrawn from service. It is seen here, now as No. 2005, at ICI's Wilton Works on 20 March 1986. Because its boiler was in such good condition, K 62005 was not scrapped. She was bought privately for preservation in 1968 and donated to the North Eastern Locomotive Preservation Group in 1972, since when, as 2005, she has undergone a major overhaul and been restored to resplendent LNER apple-green livery. In 1974, she was delivered to the North Yorkshire Moors Railway where she regularly operates passenger services.

Blue Peter is a class A2 4–6–2 locomotive, the sole surviving example of the designs of Arthur H. Peppercorn, the last Chief Mechanical Engineer of the LNER before nationalisation in 1948. In all, fifteen locomotives of this design were built; and, although *Blue Peter* was not brought into service until 25 March 1948 and had 'British Railways' on its tender, the design was LNER. Following its withdrawal from service, *Blue Peter* was stored in Scotland for more than a year, then returned to England to be stored in York. It was then purchased by Geoffrey Drury who then sent it to Doncaster for restoration, which took two years. It went on to be renamed by Valerie Singleton from the *Blue Peter* television programme. One of the largest working steam locomotives in the country, *Blue Peter* is seen here at ICI's Wilton works on 25 October 1991. It is seen but rarely these days, hauling special trains throughout the country, resplendent in BR Brunswick green livery.

With Middlesbrough separated from County Durham only by the River Tees, it is hardly surprising that posters like this one advertising its LNER dock were on display at railway stations throughout County Durham and beyond.

CHAPTER ELEVEN

EAST COAST MAIN LINE STEAM

This evocative 1930s advertisement conjures up all the mystery and excitement of journeying along the East Coast route: Lincoln's twelfth-century cathedral, which houses Great Tom, a 5-ton bell in its 265-ft high central tower; York's magnificent minster; Scarborough, 'Queen of the Yorkshire coast', with its nearby moors; Durham's glorious cathedral, unsurpassed in all Europe for its architectural splendour; Auld Reekie's Princes Street and the Scott monument; the Forth Bridge and shades of John Buchan's The Thirty-Nine Steps; *Stirling Castle, Wallace and the skirl of bagpipes; Loch Lomond; romance and adventure. To most English people in the depressed 1930s Scotland was as inaccessible as China and railway posters like this one stirred the imagination and promoted the urge to travel – and by train which, in those days, for most people, was the only practical means of doing so. Today's PR people can learn a lot from their 1930s predecessors.*

This is a stretch of the magical umbilical cord, the main East Coast Line, now electrified, between Darlington and Bradbury.

The East Coast Main Line developed from a number of smaller railways, several of which were dominated by George Hudson, known as the 'Railway King'. In 1854, the North Eastern Railway was formed from the York and North Midland, the Leeds and Northern and the York, Newcastle and Berwick. The other partners in the East Coast Route were the Great Northern from London to Doncaster and the North British from Berwick to Edinburgh and Glasgow. So the East Coast Main Line took shape. As a result of the 1923 'grouping' the three partners along the route, the Great Northern, the North Eastern and the North British were brought together as the London and North Eastern Railway. The LNER's strong links with the East Coast were brought to the public's attention through posters such as this absolutely charming portrayal of a boy and his dog frolicking at the seaside.

In 1930 passengers on the LNER not only travelled well, they also dined well in any of the company's 200 restaurant cars. The sophisticated lady seen here, with the then almost obligatory cigarette, portrays an elegance sadly considered passé today.

If some station buffets offered sandwiches with curled edges, restaurant cars on LNER expresses such as the 'Silver Jubilee' provided excellent à la carte and table d'hôte menus at reasonable prices. Had you wished to dine on the 'Silver Jubilee' on 16 September 1936, this would have been your choice of fare. The accompanying comprehensive wine list included Bass and Worthington at 8½d a bottle and special Scotch whisky at 10d per glass.

The *Silver Link*, a class A4 locomotive 4–6–2 No. 2509, was designed to run at exceptionally high speeds while giving the travelling public a special degree of comfort. It pulled the 'Silver Jubilee', the first train running on a British railway to be streamlined throughout. The locomotive's name came from the *Lay of the Last Minstrel*, Sir Walter Scott's second major work, published in 1805 – 'True love's the gift which God has given to man alone beneath heaven. It is the secret sympathy, the *silver link* which heart to heart and mind to mind, in body and in soul can bind.' The 'Silver Jubilee' was introduced to the travelling public on 27 September 1935 to celebrate the LNER's 110th birthday; and was so called in celebration of King George V's twenty-five years on the throne. It provided a 4-hour service between London and Newcastle, a distance of 268 miles, with an intermediate stop at Darlington. It was designed to run for long distances at over 70 miles an hour. Its average time between Darlington and Kings Cross was 71.65 mph and its overall speed was 67.08 mph.

When Mr Gresley was working on the streamlining design for his class A4 locomotives, the first of which was the *Silver Link*, his three foremost considerations were reducing the head resistance, lifting the steam and smoke and minimising atmospheric disturbance alongside the train. He opted for a front end fashioned like a horizontal wedge because this would cause an upwardly rising current of air to sweep past the chimney and along the boiler barrel top, and its speed would carry the steam and the smoke clear of the cab; thus lateral displacement of the atmosphere would be avoided.

This front view of the *Silver Link* shows the original streamlining with the coupling in the centre recessed and the buffers flush with the frontage. In order to give access to the smokebox, the sloped front plate is divided into two parts, the larger casing door hinged at the top and the lower one hinged at the bottom and lifting forward and downwards. No allowance was made in the streamlining to accommodate anyone working on the coupling and this led to a railwayman so doing being squashed to death. Had the buffer been standing proud, the railwayman working on the recessed coupling would have had a small chance of avoiding injury. With a flush buffer, he could not escape being squashed if the *Silver Link*'s buffers came into contact with other buffers.

The *Silver Link* is seen here in its modified streamlining with both the coupling and the buffers standing proud of the streamlined frontage. But all is not what it seems. The locomotive pictured here is actually A4 *Bittern*, a sister engine, which has been cosmetically restored by NELPG (North Eastern Locomotive Preservation Group) to represent the long since scrapped *Silver Link*. It is seen here outside No. 5 depot at ICI Wilton.

On 3 July 1938, class A4 locomotive 4–6–2 No. 4468 *Mallard* was driven at a speed of 125.8 mph between Grantham and Peterborough, thus achieving a world record for steam traction that has never been broken. This painting by Gerald Coulson captures the *Mallard*'s record-breaking run brilliantly.

North East railway enthusiasts were among the 300 passengers on the 8-coach 'Aberdeen Flyer' for its historic run between Kings Cross and Edinburgh, a distance of 392 miles. It was the longest non-stop journey ever by an excursion train in this country and *Mallard* hauled it.

Driver George Dobinson in the cabin of the *Mallard*, 11 February 1972.

It's quicker by rail! The *Mallard*, the greatest steam locomotive in the world, steaming along before the LNER locomotive was restored by the NRM (National Railway Museum) in 1983. The *Mallard* is seen here in the Sonning Cutting on the Great Western Railway as part of the locomotive exchange trials during 1948.

The *Mallard* in steam again but in a state of *déshabillé*, September 1985. Still, as every lady knows, a *svelte*, streamlined figure owes much to a good foundation.

Restored to her full glory, all steamed up and ready to show that there's life in the old girl yet! The *Mallard* at Eaglescliffe, 3 September 1988.

Because of his great contribution to railways, both as an engineer and as a locomotive designer, Mr Gresley received a knighthood in 1937; so it was appropriate that the 100th class A4 'Pacific' locomotive 4–6–2 No. 4498, and built to his design, should be named *Sir Nigel Gresley* in his honour. Like others of its class, *Sir Nigel Gresley* was built to haul non-stop trains between London and the northern cities on the LNER system. It was streamlined for maximum efficiency when travelling at high speed. Taken together, locomotive and tender were 71 ft long and weighed about 167 tons. The driving wheels were 6 ft 8 in in diameter and were driven from these three cylinders actuated by Gresley's derived valve motion.

Hauling a 'Steam Safari' train, *Sir Nigel Gresley* roars out of Newcastle Central, belching smoke and steam, 19 June 1972. It, and others of its class, were expected to travel some 75,000 miles between major overhauls.

Sir Nigel Gresley is resplendent in its LNER livery of garter blue, a magnificent specimen speeding through the countryside, 3 April 1938. Mileage records ceased to be kept after 1962, but it is estimated that *Sir Nigel Gresley* travelled some 2 million miles in revenue-earning service. In 1957, while hauling a private excursion, *Sir Nigel Gresley* reached a speed of 113 mph between Grantham and Peterborough. Later, when in private ownership, *Sir Nigel Gresley* hauled a special 385-ton train over Shap Fell, in Westmorland, at a faster time than had previously been recorded.

Darlington-built LNER locomotive 10000 *Hush Hush* 4–6–4 at Durham station, *c.* 1935. This locomotive did yeoman service hauling express passenger trains between Kings Cross and Newcastle.

Darlington-built LNER locomotive 10000 *Hush Hush* seen in its original streamlined design, November 1933. The boiler was not satisfactory for rail use.

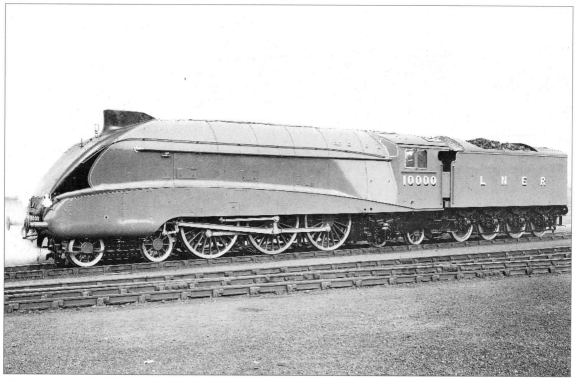

Hush Hush was taken out of service, rebuilt and streamlined to a much improved design. It is seen here after the transformation, 25 November 1937.

Poetry in motion! LNER class A4 'Pacific' locomotive No. 60021 4–6–2 *Wild Swan* hauling 'The Talisman' between Edinburgh and Kings Cross, mid-1950s.

'The Elizabethan' hauled by A4 'Pacific' No. 60028 *Walter K. Whigham*, passing Aycliffe on the way to Edinburgh, 29 June 1953.

This photograph of 'The North Briton' at speed in July 1952 captures the age of railway steam at its magnificent best. It evokes all the romance and the thrill of thundering through the countryside hauled by a powerful steam locomotive.

A4 Gresley 'Pacifics' were not confined to express passenger train service. Here No. 60019 *Bittern*, sister to the *Mallard*, is pictured hauling a freight train at York, on 6 September 1966.

The *Golden Eagle*, No. 4482, first of the new LNER streamlined super 'Pacific' locomotives that would draw the 'Coronation' expresses, is steaming out of Kings Cross, bound for Newcastle, 27 January 1937. This was its first test tun.

Later that year, on 9 July, this 'Coronation' streamlined express is photographed moving out of York station on its first run north. 'Coronation' expresses were usually pulled by 'Dominion' class streamlined 'Pacifics'.

'The Elizabethan' express is passing through Darlington on its way north, pulled by A4 'Pacific' No. 60028 *Walter K. Whigham*, 29 June 1953.

The express flyer 'The Fair Maid' photographed arriving at Darlington Bank Top station *en route* from Kings Cross to Perth, 17 September 1957. Pulling it is A4 'Pacific' No. 60015 *Quicksilver*.

An express pulled by an A4 'Pacific' is thundering past the diesel depot at Darlington at full speed, 21 January 1960. The cooling towers in the background have since been demolished.

The A4 'Pacific' No. 60009 *Union of South Africa* arrives in Newcastle Central pulling an express lugubriously called 'Jubilee Requiem', 24 October 1964. When, on 27 September 1935, Britain's first streamlined train came into service, Sir Ralph Wedgwood, Chief General Manager of the LNER, in a speech made before the start of a special run by the *Silver Link* between Kings Cross and Grantham, pointed out that 110 years earlier to the very day the first passenger train in the world had run between Darlington and Stockton. Sir Ralph emphasised that the high level of speed would not be attained at the expense of safety and that passengers would take no greater risk travelling on the streamlined expresses than on the 'Flying Scotsman'. He drew attention to the fact that speed had not increased correspondingly with locomotive power because of the ever-increasing weight of the carriages. He regarded the streamlined train as a novel business experiment, which he hoped would receive public support.

The *Union of South Africa* was the last A4 to run non-stop from Kings Cross to Edinburgh; and when it arrived in Newcastle was 53 minutes late. On the return trip it was 2 minutes late leaving Newcastle but, by covering 80 miles in 80 minutes, it reached York 3 minutes early. Attaining a maximum speed of 96 mph it reached Kings Cross 26 minutes early. The round trip was called 'Jubilee Requiem' because it was the last chance for anyone to ride behind an A4. When the *Union of South Africa* left Kings Cross station for the engine shed the driver blew a prolonged blast on the whistle.

A rare picture of three class A4 'Pacific' locomotives taken at a rail weekend at York, 3 July 1988. From left to right are *Sir Nigel Gresley*, converted *Silver Link* and *Mallard*, all of which saw regular service along the East Coast Route.

There was a darker side to the development of the railways. Countless setbacks included derailments and collisions, some with fatal consequences. The years took their toll and a number of both railway workers and passengers were maimed or killed. On 15 November 1910, there was a collision at Darlington's Bank Top station, pictured here, which toppled an engine and tender unit.

This collision occurred in Darlington Bank Top station on 9 March 1929. Two people were killed as a result.

On 15 June 1938, C.G. Ferguson, then head boy of Durham School, drove locomotive No. 60860 *Durham School* out of the now defunct Elvet station, Durham City, at the start of its twenty-five years of proud service. During that time it travelled almost a million miles, mostly on the London–Scottish line. The Darlington-built *Durham School* was designed by Sir Nigel Gresley; and when it was withdrawn from service in 1963, the engine's nameplate was handed over to Mr John Brett, the school's headmaster, by Mr P.B. Johnson, District Passenger Superintendent, British Railways. In this picture A.J. Bower, right, head boy of Durham School in 1963, shows the nameplate to other pupils.

Durham Light Infantry cadets alongside the locomotive named after their famous regiment, 19 June, 1961.

This plaque was fixed to a diesel locomotive named after the Durham Light Infantry to commemorate the bicentenary of the raising of the regiment in 1758.

K1 2–6–0 No. 2005 pulling 'the North Eastern' out of Stockton station, 23 April 1979. In 1949 the first class K1 locomotives type 2–6–0 were introduced. They were a simplified development of Sir Nigel Gresley's three-cylinder K4, which had been specially built for the arduous West Highland Line in Glasgow by the North British Locomotive Company. All the K1s were built between 1949 and 1950, No. 62005 (later becoming No. 2005) being outshopped in June 1949. Her entire working life was spent in the north-east of England and in 1968 she was bought privately for preservation. In 1972, she was donated by the owners to the North Eastern Locomotive Preservation Group. Following major overhaul and having been restored to her LNER apple-green livery she was delivered to the North Yorkshire Moors Railway where she hauls passenger trains as No. 2005.

K1 No. 2005 is seen twelve years later, steaming out of Darlington Bank Top station, 'fit as a flea and all set to run again', 28 March 1993.

Long before Sir Nigel Gresley's K1 was thought of, the locomotive considered by many to be the most famous of them all was built. The year was 1923 and the locomotive was the *Flying Scotsman*, class A3 type 4–6–2 No. 1472. Constructed soon after the formation of the LNER, it was the third of a new class of A1 'Pacifics'. In all seventy-eight locomotives of this class were built, providing the LNER with first-class motive power on its main lines. All A1 locomotives were built to class A3 design with higher pressure boilers and other improvements. Each locomotive had a name, mostly from famous racehorses. The tender on the *Flying Scotsman* had a corridor running right through it to enable the driver and firemen to be changed *en route* while working the train non-stop between London and Edinburgh, a distance of 393 miles. By means of a scoop situated beneath the tender, which could be lowered into water troughs positioned between the rails, it was possible to pick up water while the train was in motion, thus allowing greater distances to be covered without stopping for that purpose. The tender held enough coal to cover 400 miles. On 1 May 1928, locomotive No. 1472, now renumbered No. 4472, left Kings Cross for Edinburgh at 10 a.m. pulling the first non-stop run of the 'Flying Scotsman' express, after which it had been named. This famous train still leaves Kings Cross for Edinburgh at 10 a.m. daily, but now it is hauled by a diesel-electric locomotive and makes an intermediate stop at Newcastle. In 1934, when pulling a test train, the *Flying Scotsman* attained a speed of 100 mph on a 1 in 200 down gradient and more than 82 mph going up the same gradient on the return run. During its working life the *Flying Scotsman* travelled 2,080 miles. It was withdrawn from service on 14 January 1963, by which time it had a British Railways number, 60103. But to the world and his wife, this magnificent locomotive will always be remembered as the *Flying Scotsman*.

The *Flying Scotsman*, now owned by Mr Alan Pegler, leaving Darlington, 9 March 1965. Having been overhauled, it was at the start of a trial run, after which it was painted in its former LNER colours. When the *Flying Scotsman* was withdrawn from service it carried a double chimney and German type smoke deflectors. It was immediately restored at Darlington's North Road Works.

On 1 May 1968, the *Flying Scotsman*, by now forty-five years old, repeated the non-stop run from Kings Cross to Edinburgh. The next year, following a complete overhaul, it made an extensive tour of North America, complete with bell and cow-catcher. On its return, it was again restored to its original condition and painted in the famous apple-green livery of the LNER.

Cock of the North, having just been completed at the Doncaster Works of the LNER for service between Aberdeen, Edinburgh and Carlisle, 16 May 1934. Although its link with Durham may appear tenuous, it is necessary to compare the opposition in order to get a more balanced picture of the railway network as a whole. In the mid–1930s, this new streamlined locomotive *Cock of the North* was considered to be the most powerful passenger locomotive in the British Isles.

LNER class A3 4–6–2 locomotive No. 2750 *Papyrus* leaving Kings Cross with a full head of steam, 5 March 1935. There is a dynamometer car immediately behind the tender. Driven by H. Gutteridge, it had travelled non-stop from Kings Cross to Newcastle. On the return trip, driven by W. Sparshott, a speed of 105 mph was reached on the descent of Stoke Bank, and a little further on 108 mph was attained. *Papyrus* covered the distance between Newcastle and Kings Cross in 231 minutes 41 seconds, a feat that set the scene for the next Gresley 'Pacific' class A4.

BR locomotive No. 70,000 type 4–6–2 *Britannia*, which came into service in 1951, the year this photograph was taken, was one of a series of locomotives built to replace the ageing classes of the old companies. All the old works and drawing offices had a hand in its design and the objective was efficiency and ease of maintenance. The wheels were completely uncovered and the valve gear was outside but, despite this, all the 'Britannia' class engines, the first of the 'Standards', looked, and indeed were, very powerful engines. However, the crews had mixed feelings about them. While they could appreciate the motives behind the design, some crews, in particular ex-GWR men, were unhappy because the locomotives were not pure products of their Swindon works. Despite their hybrid design, the 'Brits' did yeoman work wherever they were needed, be it pulling the 'Golden Arrow' on the Southern Region or hauling other main line expresses along the East Coast Line.

A contrast in styles: *Mallard* class A4 4–6–2, famed for pulling expresses at very high speeds, stands alongside class 4 No. 76025 type 2–6–0, a locomotive used for hauling mixed traffic.

When Arthur H. Peppercorn, the last Chief Mechanical Engineer of the LNER before nationalisation in 1948, succeeded Edward Thompson, who had designed and built three different designs of the 4–6–2 locomotive, he made certain changes to the outstanding orders. He did so because Edward Thompson had made radical changes to the early Gresley designs, not all the details of which were successful. Fifteen locomotives were built at Doncaster, all of which retained a number of standard parts, and subsequently a further design was produced, the A1, which had larger driving wheels than the A2. *Flamboyant*, pictured here on 22 November 1962, was one of these. This magnificent locomotive, No. 60153, saw service on the East Coast Route.

North Eastern No. 60147 was another A1 'Pacific'. No matter which way you view these superb locomotives, they look good and exude power.

Considered by many to be the most graceful locomotive ever built, this class 'Sterling Single' locomotive No. 53 type 4–2–2 the *Flying Scotsman* was designed by Patrick Sterling. The sweeping curves of the smokebox flow smoothly around the cylinders and the top of the boiler does not have the customary steam dome. Known as 'eight footers' because of the diameter of their driving wheels, the later locomotives were 50 per cent more powerful than the prototype and pulled the principal East Coast expresses until after the end of the nineteenth century. Stirlings like the *Flying Scotsman* took part in races to the north in 1888 and 1895. The 'Flying Scotsman' symbolised East Coast express passenger motive power with locomotives like the *Flying Scotsman*, seen here, *Henry Oakley* and *Sir Nigel Gresley*.

A Great Northern dining car, as pulled by the *Flying Scotsman, c.* 1900.

The first occasion on which wireless telephone communication was made between a train and an aeroplane, 20 May 1932. The LNER 'Flying Scotsman' and the airliner *Hercules* near Newark, Notts, where the tests took place.

Passengers lean out of the carriage windows as the *Flying Scotsman* passes under Cockton Hill railway bridge, Bishop Auckland, on 10 September 1967.

LNER class V2 type 2–6–2 No. 4771 *Green Arrow* at Bank Top station, Darlington, 11 July 1987. This locomotive was one of five built in 1936 to meet the ever-increasing demands of the day for fast and reliable mixed-traffic locomotives. The design embodied many of the successful features of early Gresley designs and the 6 ft 2 in driving wheels and a very efficient boiler and cylinder assembly made these locomotives very popular for both express passenger and freight work. No. 4771 regularly hauled the 3.55 p.m. 'Scottish Goods' along the East Coast Route from London. The V2 locomotive, referred to by the LNER crews as 'the locomotives that won the war', could work as well as the larger 'Pacific' locomotives.

Driver Rodney Lytton with the *Green Arrow* in steam for the last time before being overhauled, 5 September 1992. V2s worked on all the main routes of the LNER until the early 1960s when the new diesel-electric locomotives made them redundant originally. When *Green Arrow* was withdrawn from service it was completely overhauled and repainted in the LNER livery of apple green.

During the 1930s, railway speeds on the East Coast Main Line began to rise. In 1934 and 1935, the LNER did some test runs with the *Flying Scotsman* and *Papyrus* recording speeds of 100 and 108 mph. Following the success of the LNER trial runs in 1935, the first of the streamliners, the 'Silver Jubilee' express was introduced. It ran non-stop between Darlington and Kings Cross, averaging 70.4 mph in both directions over the 232.3 miles, making it the fastest long-distance train in the world. On 27 September 1935, hauled by *Silver Link*, 'Silver Jubilee' eclipsed all previous speeds achieved on rails in this country. This paved the way for other high-speed trains and in 1937 the second of the East Coast streamlined expresses, the 'Coronation', ran between London and Edinburgh in 6 hours. Its speed of 71.9 mph booked over the 188.2 miles between Kings Cross and York was the fastest yet to appear on a British timetable. The LMS introduced the *Coronation Scot* and set up a new British railway speed record of 114 mph. The LNER's chance to regain the rail speed record came in July 1938 during brake tests with *Mallard*, when the world speed record for steam locomotives was broken. At the summit of Stoke Bank the train touched 74 mph, 6 miles later

the speed was up to 116 mph and it peaked at 126 mph. This feat was never beaten in the steam era. Behind *Mallard*'s success were the driver and fireman who drove it. Their pride is reflected in the faces of those who followed in their footsteps, such as Ivor Nadin and Jackie Hatch, seen here in the cab of *Mallard*, 29 August 1988.

BR class K1, first introduced in 1949, was a simplified development of Sir Nigel Gresley's three-cylinder K4, especially built in 1937 for the arduous West Highland Line. One of six K4s was reconstructed in 1945 with just two outside cylinders to lessen maintenance by Mr E. Thompson, Chief Mechanical Engineer of the LNER. The experiment was a success and Mr A.H. Peppercorn, Mr Thompson's successor, ordered a further seventy for mixed-traffic duties both in the Highlands of Scotland and throughout eastern England. K1 No. 2005 type 2–6–0, seen here pulling 'The North Eastern' on 22 April 1979, was out-shopped in June 1949 and spent all its working life in the north-east of England.

Sir Nigel Gresley hauling the 'Tyne-Tees Pullman' on the approach to Darlington's Bank Top station during the nostalgia trip to Kings Cross, June 1995. The overhead wires are evidence that electricity has usurped steam as motive power.

As the golden age of railway steam becomes part of history, LMS class 5MT type 4–6–0 *George Stephenson* takes part in the bicentenary celebrations of George Stephenson's birth in the pretty Tyneside village of Wylam, 7 June 1981. Seen here pulling a 'George Stephenson Birthday Special', this fine locomotive, often described as the most successful class ever built by the LMS, was first introduced in 1934. It was withdrawn from service in 1967 because of the coming of the end of steam. Although not used on the East Coast Line, its name is inextricably linked to the history of Durham Railways. Perhaps the band is playing 'Coronation Scot'.

The first day run of the high-speed diesel 'The Talisman' had an inconspicuous beginning in June 1964. A steam locomotive was used to tow it into and out of Darlington Bank Top station.

But the day belonged to 'The Talisman'. It travelled the 232 miles from Darlington to Kings Cross that auspicious summer day in 1964 at an average speed of 67.2 mph. Even though at one time it was running 7 minutes late, the 3,300 hp Deltic diesel locomotive arrived at Kings Cross 15 seconds before 2.15 p.m., the time it was due to arrive. It pulled eight special coaches, imaginatively named Project XP 64, and it looked like a train that went like a rocket. So luxurious was this two-tone blue train that when it reached Edinburgh for the start of its first ever passenger service, those passengers booked second class thought that every carriage was first class. With 'The Talisman' the Deltic era had arrived.

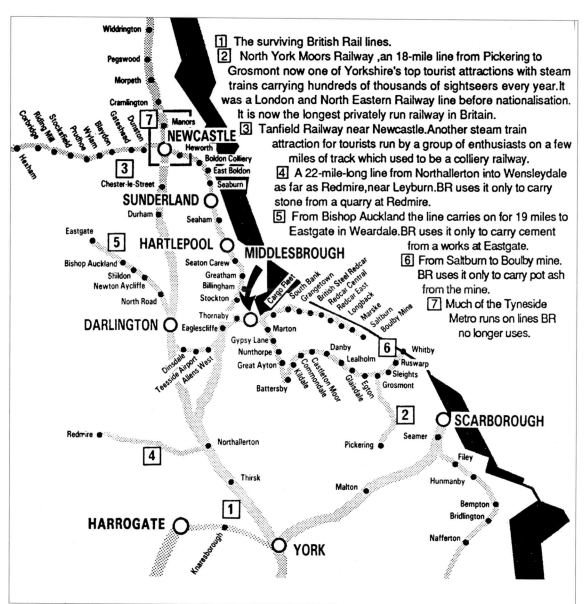

The map contains the following labels and key:

1. The surviving British Rail lines.
2. North York Moors Railway, an 18-mile line from Pickering to Grosmont now one of Yorkshire's top tourist attractions with steam trains carrying hundreds of thousands of sightseers every year. It was a London and North Eastern Railway line before nationalisation. It is now the longest privately run railway in Britain.
3. Tanfield Railway near Newcastle. Another steam train attraction for tourists run by a group of enthusiasts on a few miles of track which used to be a colliery railway.
4. A 22-mile-long line from Northallerton into Wensleydale as far as Redmire, near Leyburn. BR uses it only to carry stone from a quarry at Redmire.
5. From Bishop Auckland the line carries on for 19 miles to Eastgate in Weardale. BR uses it only to carry cement from a works at Eastgate.
6. From Saltburn to Boulby mine. BR uses it only to carry pot ash from the mine.
7. Much of the Tyneside Metro runs on lines BR no longer uses.

Nationalisation marked the beginning of British Rail and was regarded by many as a cause for celebration. Now the railway was owned by the people – but try taking some of your own coal from a railway stock pile and you are in trouble! – and grand steam trains huffing and puffing into stations were greeted by cheering platform workers waving their caps. When the Labour government of the day took over Britain's four main private railway companies, along with other smaller ones, it inherited an empire. In the forty years between nationalisation and the end of the Deltic era Britain's massive railway network was decimated: 635,000 staff were reduced to 100,000 employees, 52,000 miles of track, enough to circle the world twice, became 24,477 miles, and 20,000 steam engines, 40,000 carriages and more than 1,200,000 wagons were reduced to a small fraction of those numbers. County Durham was left with just the main line from London to Edinburgh, with trains passing through Darlington and Durham, together with a few branch lines. It was during the 1960s that most of the branch lines were closed by Dr Richard 'Axe Man' Beeching. This map shows the few remaining lines.

CHAPTER TWELVE

THE DELTIC ERA

The Deltic era covered the fifteen years from 1962 until 1977 and is best remembered for the vast physical changes on the East Coast Main Line brought about by a new confidence and management style. The self doubt of the Marples-Beeching era was being replaced by an outgoing, aggressive organisation which was marketing an excellent national product called Inter City. British Rail's marketing people were becoming customer, rather than product, orientated. Diesel was replacing steam, new passenger coaches were being built and there was a lot of investment in track and signalling. The outstanding LNER achievements of the 1930s were being gradually eclipsed by the new norms of the 1960s. During the 1970s the average time of all daytime trains between Kings Cross and Edinburgh was less than 6 hours. The experimental Deltic, seen here in November 1958, which was built at English Electric's Preston Works, made its appearance in 1956 and was tried out exhaustively for several years on both the West and East Coast Main Lines. It weighed 106 tons and was intended for both main line passenger and freight duty at a maximum speed of 90 mph, but could be geared for higher speeds. It had a driving cab at each end, was powered by two Napier engines and could develop 3,300 hp.

The 3,300 hp Deltic diesel locomotive undergoing clearance tests at Darlington, 23 October 1959.

The 'Flying Scotsman' drawn by a 2,000 hp diesel–electric locomotive, passing through Darlington at 70 mph *en route* to Edinburgh, 25 August 1958.

The Railway Queen, Hazel Dobinson, inaugurates the first diesel-electric locomotive to be built at the North Road shops Darlington, 21 January 1960.

A class 55 Deltic in full throttle thundering through a cutting south of Darlington, seen in the distance, 11 September 1961. The train covered the 232 miles from Darlington to Kings Cross in under 4 hours. The '1A03' at the front of the Deltic informs us that, 1: this is a first-class passenger express; A: it is London-bound from outside the region; 03: it is the third train of the day of its type on this route.

Here the record-breaking class 55 Deltic No. D9005 is standing in Darlington Bank Top station, June 1962. Just 4 hours later it was in Kings Cross.

At the end of the record-breaking run Deltic D9005 stands in Kings Cross, its crew, on the platform alongside it, looking as though they don't believe they've done it.

The 'Flying Scotsman' travelling through Darlington northbound and in celebration of its centenary run, 18 June 1962. The 'Flying Scotsman' was originally called 'The Scotch Express'.

The southbound 'Tyne Tees Pullman' on the outskirts of Darlington, 18 June 1962. By this time the railways had changed dramatically from pre-Second World War days when railway publicity promoted two themes: the romance of a journey by a crack steam-hauled express and the railway's part in the family holiday to the seaside, probably the only occasion when the average family made a long train journey. In the 1960s, faced with stiff competition from widespread private car ownership, coach tours and package air tours abroad, British Rail had to develop new ways of selling itself. Of these, the most important was the choice of Inter City as a national brand name which was publicised nationally in TV commercials and in press and poster campaigns.

The 'Queen of Scots' express leaving Darlington on its last day of service, 13 June 1964. It arrived in Darlington at 1642 and departed at 1645. The following day, *Pullman* became *Talisman* and this service was removed the following April.

The last of the Deltics just before the introduction of the High Speed Train, January 1972.

The Deltic is pulling Mark II coaches, the interior of which is seen here, 1964. These coaches were introduced in 1964 and looked exactly like the Mark IIA. Three years later, in 1967, Mark IIA main line passenger coaches came into service bringing the latest in luxury. At first glance there were cries of 'What's the difference?', but closer inspection revealed those facets that have made the Mark IIA such an improvement on the conventional passenger coach. The second-class coaches incorporated double-glazed windows, improved insulation, thermostatically controlled pressure heating and ventilation as well as individual reading lights, strategically placed and guaranteed not to cause a shadow. Improvements to the first-class coaches included extensively glazed, easy moving compartment doors and background fluorescent lighting supplementing individual lighting over the seats.

A naval officer, Captain Joe Slater, seated in the cab of a Class 50 at Newcastle has a valid explanation. When, in May 1982, HMS *Illustrious* was launched at Swan Hunters the event was commemorated by naming this Class 50, No. 50037, *Illustrious*.

Captain Joe Slater of HMS *Illustrious* at the naming ceremony of No. 50037. On the left is John Thomson, British Railway's Divisional Manager.

It is 9 July 1988 and change is in the air. This class 47/4 diesel at Castle Hill Junction, Northallerton, passes posts erected to carry electric power lines which are not yet in position. It marks another step in the electrification of the line, the shape of things to come.

Improved train speeds on the East Coast Main Line and elsewhere were achieved through signalling and engineering projects. A new signalling centre for Tyneside, an artist's impression of which is seen here, was built in Askew Road, Gateshead, by Shepherd Construction Ltd of York at a cost of almost £1 million. The centre controls the 120 miles of main line between Northallerton and the Scottish border and several branch lines. Push buttons change both points and signals to set up complete routes for approaching trains; and the station announcer, who has a full view of the train movements depicted by colour lights on the panel, broadcasts the latest information on arrivals and departures. It cleared the way for electric trains running between Kings Cross and Edinburgh from May 1991.

Following many years of building steam locomotives, the first diesel-electric to be built at Darlington was D5094, seen here setting out on a trial run, 9 February 1960.

Driver Bill Jones has his hand on the throttle as the speedometer on the right registers 100 mph, 15 April 1966. He is on a press review run and about to pass a goods train hauled by an old fashioned steam locomotive, four days before British Railways Midland Region's crack new electrified services between London and the north-west were inaugurated. The electric locomotive is one of the most powerful on British Rail and takes its power from the overhead line. It is on a fast stretch of track near Crewe; but it is a scene soon to be repeated in many other areas including the East Coast Main Line.

CHAPTER THIRTEEN

TOWARDS TOMORROW WITH HST125 AND IC225

The Mark II passenger coach, introduced during 1964, early in the Deltic era, brought the latest in luxury travel; and it is still in use on many routes. In 1971 it was superseded by the Mark IID which, with its air-conditioning and automatic doors between the coaches, represented the most up-to-date stock on British railways to date. All Inter City 125 sets are made up with Mark IIIs. Here an Inter City train of air-conditioned coaches is on the East Coast Main Line, north of York, northbound for County Durham and beyond.

The Inter City 125 is so named because it can run up to that speed in miles per hour. Thus, a first-class passenger in a Mark IID coach such as the one seen here, part of an Inter City express, enjoys a standard of luxury rail travel previously unavailable while being whisked to his destination. The otherwise admirable air-conditioning of the Mark IID was at times affected by the smell of the brakes, which was sucked in and distributed throughout the train. This fault was rectified in the even more advanced Mark IV coach, which will be standard well into the twenty-first century.

This prototype of a new breed of High Speed Train, class 252, left Kings Cross at 8.15 a.m. on 27 September 1975 on a proving run. On board was HRH the Duke of Edinburgh *en route* to open first the National Railway Museum at York, then the North Road Railway Museum at Darlington. On the proving run it captured the world speed record for diesel powered trains, running at 143 mph.

Heading south to pass the halfway mark between Edinburgh and London, south of Darlington, 20 March 1978.

High Speed Train No. 254005 at Darlington Bank Top station, northbound, 15 May 1979. Unlike crack expresses in some other countries, which are usually for first-class passengers only or have a supplement added to the fare, Inter City is for everyone at the ordinary fare or reduced rate without a supplement.

When the new class 158 locomotive, British Rail Provincial's new 90 mph air-conditioned luxury diesel train, was introduced, drivers learned to drive it with the help of a train simulator. It is housed inside the bus.

Inside the bus, BR Traction Inspector Karl Watts is at the simulator controls preparing to take his 'train' out of York's station, a journey completed with the aid of computers.

This is the real thing, the class 158 sprinter, on test along the Newcastle to Liverpool route at the south end of Crimple Viaduct, Harrogate. The class 158 operates on Provincial's network of express routes and on other inter-urban routes including the East Coast Main Line through Durham. This publicity shot was taken in 1991.

Councillor Jim Skinner, Mayor of Darlington, at Bank Top station, Darlington, naming an Inter City – you've guessed it – *Darlington*, May 1984.

The revived 'Tyne-Tees Pullman' being waved off by the Mayor and Mayoress as it leaves Newcastle Central three days before entering public service, Friday 27 September 1985. It formed a specially prepared HST and sped from Newcastle to Kings Cross in 2 hours 19 minutes. Its average speed was 115.4 mph which it attained travelling through Essendine. The power car is No. E43038.

Same day, same run, same HST. Exactly 160 years since the opening of the S&DR and exactly 50 years since the record-breaking run of the 'Silver Jubilee' HST power car No. E43038 passes the National Railway Museum at York where A4 No. 4468 *Mallard*, in steam but without its streamlined casing, is in the company of GNR No. 1.

Swallow, the first electric locomotive to use the East Coast Line, at Darlington Bank Top station, 11 May 1991.

This Inter City standing at Darlington Bank Top station is about to make a special run to Peterborough, 2 June 1995. It is a shortened train propelled by No. 91031 *Sir Henry Royce*. Inter City managers had decided to have a crack at the British passenger carrier record. The crosses on the buffers indicate that the train is attempting to break a speed record and that, as far as possible, adjacent lines have been cleared of traffic. During the run 154.1 mph was recorded at Stoke Bank. The record was broken.

Two Inter City 225s about to pass near Peterborough, 22 June 1995. The one on the left is propelled by No. 91031 *Sir Henry Royce* on its record-beating run.

On Monday 8 July 1991, the Inter City trains, brand new to the East Coast Main Line, began running to a new timetable, offering the fastest ever journey on the route from Kings Cross to Newcastle, Edinburgh and Glasgow. These new electrics are called Inter City 225 because they can run at 225 kph, which is 140 mph. Their brand image is a swallow and this appears on the trains as well as the publicity material, for example, the route map. There are twenty-seven trains each way every day between Newcastle and Kings Cross, offering more than 27,000 seats. The fastest train completes the journey in 2 hours 41 minutes and nine others make the 269-mile trip in less than 3 hours. Newcastle's very own Pullman train to London, the 'Newcastle Pullman', leaves at 0700 daily, stops only at Durham and arrives in London at 0945; and it represents the highest standards of catering and personal attention for Inter City business travellers. Inter City No. 91011, seen here in a publicity shot, is speeding northwards towards Durham and points north. This publicity shot was taken in July 1991.

Inter City No. 91025 is seen speeding southwards, down the Northumberland coast, towards Durham and the south. Each Inter City 225 comprises nine passenger vehicles and is powered by a class 91 locomotive at one end of the train and with a Driving Van Trailer (DVT), including a driving cab, at the other end. With a maximum power output of 6300 hp and a top speed of 140 mph (225 kph) the class 91 is the fastest and most powerful locomotive ever to run in Britain. After nearly ten years of service all the Inter City 225 locomotives are being rebuilt internally.

Durham City, with its magnificent cathedral, prominent in the middle distance and an HST Inter City 125 on the viaduct in the foreground, faithfully captures the very essence of Durham Railways.

BRITAIN IN OLD PHOTOGRAPHS

SUTTON'S PHOTOGRAPHIC HISTORY OF TRANSPORT

To order any of these titles please telephone our distributor, Littlehampton Book Services on 01903 828800
For a catalogue of these and our other titles please ring Emma Leitch on 01453 731114